BERKLEE GUITAR THEORY

Kim Perlak
CURATOR

Developed by the
Berklee Guitar
Department
Faculty

BERKLEE PRESS

Editor in Chief: Jonathan Feist
Senior Vice President of Online Learning and Continuing Education/CEO of Berklee Online: Debbie Cavalier
Editorial Assistant: Brittany McCorriston
Author Photo: Jonathan Feist

Advisors: Larry Baione and Sheryl Bailey
Studies by Members of the Berklee Guitar Department Education Committee
Music Notation Assistant: Ian Steed

ISBN 978-0-87639-218-8

Berklee
Press

1140 Boylston Street • MS-855BP
Boston, MA 02215-3693 USA

Visit Berklee Press Online at
www.berkleepress.com

Berklee Online

Study music online at
online.berklee.edu

DISTRIBUTED BY

HAL•LEONARD®

7777 W. BLUEMOUND RD. P.O. BOX 13819
MILWAUKEE, WISCONSIN 53213

Visit Hal Leonard Online
www.halleonard.com

Berklee Press, a publishing activity of Berklee College of Music, is a not-for-profit educational publisher.
Available proceeds from the sales of our products are contributed to the scholarship funds of the college.

CONTENTS

ACKNOWLEDGMENTS

This book is made possible by the dedication, creativity, and expertise of the Berklee College of Music Guitar Department faculty and chairs, who worked tirelessly to build our department and shape our pedagogy since the 1960s. Thank you to our late professor Mick Goodrick; Larry Baione, chair emeritus; and Rick Peckham, professor and former assistant chair; for guiding the revisions that shaped our current department curriculum. Thank you to Larry Baione and Sheryl Bailey, assistant chair, for their advising on this book.

Thank you to our full-time faculty who serve on the Berklee Guitar Department Education Committee for their contributions to this book, and for their work each day with our students. Thank you to our alumni Rihards Kolmanis, Andres Guerra, Quincy Cotton, and Roy Ben Bashat for their work preparing the musical examples. Thank you to our Berklee Press editor, Jonathan Feist, for his patience as we put together and revised this volume of work.

The Berklee Guitar Department is a global community of alumni, faculty, students, staff, visiting artists, and colleagues whose work and experience inspire us and push us to develop our work and artistry in our Boston classrooms and beyond. Thank you all.

PREFACE

At Berklee College of Music and around the world, our Guitar Department is known for its deep and comprehensive approach to theory on our instrument. Since the 1960s, our faculty and chairs have worked together to compile this curricular material, consisting of fundamentals, scales, chords, arpeggios, and reading examples that players need in order to know the instrument and build a foundation in any style. Members of our department community will recognize this material as the "proficiency" or "final exam" material, which is organized into eight levels of exams for our students to perform at the end of each semester.

Rather than approaching theory in a conceptual manner, the Berklee guitar proficiency presents practical applications—"where to put your fingers"—to create a musical vocabulary on our instrument. Beginning with the fundamentals of basic technique, note location, and rhythm, our vocabulary list grows exponentially to make connections across the fingerboard. We begin with these fundamentals in our pedagogy (and in daily practice) to remind ourselves that our minds, hands, ears, and hearts must remain connected throughout the learning process. For this reason, the proficiency material is connected to the private lesson at Berklee—where our faculty guide students through these lessons and make connections to their creative work. As an accompaniment to these vocabulary lessons, we encourage constant cross-referencing to stylistic applications and theoretical concepts—such as those provided in chapter 7, "Studies." These examples in the "Studies" chapter are written by members of our current faculty Guitar Education Committee and our chair emeritus, Larry Baione.

This book is intended to serve as both an introduction to and a review of our current Guitar Department core proficiency materials. Current members of our community will find familiar fingerings and explanations, and notice that there are some concepts that reflect the developing nature of the proficiencies.

To use this book, take time each day to come back to the early chapters—even as you are working through the later lessons. Practice the examples given, and then take the suggestions to apply this instruction to all keys and explore the referenced materials. Bring these foundational materials to your lessons, rehearsals, and into your creative work in your personal style. None of us will ever graduate from these fundamentals on our instrument—ten, twenty, thirty, forty—fifty years from now— you will find as we have: that the learning and application of this material is a beautiful life-long pursuit.

Remember: to be the musicians we are on the guitar, we have our hearts, our ears, our minds, our hands, and our instruments as our expressive tools. Our strategy as your faculty is to provide the foundational materials and instruction that allows each and all of us to create our personal music on our shared instrument.

We're in this together.

Welcome to the Guitar Department.

Kim Perlak

Chair, Guitar

Berklee College of Music, March 2023

ABOUT THIS BOOK

Background of the Proficiency at Berklee College of Music

The Berklee Guitar Department was founded in 1962, and has had four chairs: Jack Peterson (1962 to 1965), William Leavitt (1965 to 1990), Larry Baione (1990 to 2018), and myself, Kim Perlak (2018 to the present). As the first collegiate guitar department to offer a degree, and the first to offer concentrations in styles other than classical music, the chairs and faculty committed to creating a curriculum on the instrument. As the department grew and expanded to include all styles of guitar, this curriculum focused on foundational materials that would allow players to be both versatile and deep in their knowledge of our instrument. The resulting and ever-developing collection of materials is known as the "proficiency" or the "final exam" material. For the final exams each semester, this material is organized into eight levels of tests. Students work on this material with faculty in their private lessons, and apply it in labs, ensembles, and creative work.

Much of the current proficiency's development took place under the chair leadership of Bill Leavitt and Larry Baione, with significant contributions made by former assistant chair Rick Peckham and professor Mick Goodrick.

Now serving as chair emeritus, Larry Baione shares his perspective on this evolution:

The idea of the proficiencies, which we now call the final exams, is about learning the guitar—to be used in any style. One of the focuses of the Guitar Department has been for guitarists to be working musicians. Over the years, as faculty were hired from different stylistic and professional backgrounds, the proficiencies morphed to reflect that. As the years went on, for example, we added reading due to the fact that guitar instruction pre-Berklee—if it wasn't formalized—didn't always include that.

All the scales and their modes—major, melodic minor, harmonic minor, harmonic major, etc.—are used in improv in music we'll come across. The fingerings we use for both the chords and the scales give us a way of getting to things—learning patterns that are comfortable gives us a way to play the guitar well and get a good sound. It gives us choices as to where to play melodies. It allows you to master your instrument.

Students ask, "Why do I have to learn scales in position?" Well, that's only the beginning. After a while, the fingerboard becomes one big position. You take these two-octave patterns and learn to connect them; when I teach the three-octave scales, I say you should practice switching on every string. As we all get more advanced, we notice that chords are scales, and scales are chords. They're all related.

When I arrived as a student in 1967, Bill Leavitt was the chair, and everyone had to take all the proficiencies at some point before graduation. There was one "famous" person who didn't take any until his last week at Berklee. He took all eight levels with Bill, and he was in there over an hour and a half. The proficiencies started to be part of the lesson grade for each student each semester around 1985, and that's when they became final exams.

When I was a student, each of us wrote and performed a chord solo. We learned commonly used right-hand rhythms. Bill Leavitt played a lot of shows, and he knew what was required to work in that context. We also learned and performed a Bach invention or another classical piece with a pick—everything was performed with a pick in those days. That was something we changed very quickly in the proficiency revisions—that you didn't need to play with a pick to study at Berklee. As the department grew, we allowed the proficiencies to morph in order to allow players to work in the different styles that became reflected.

The material shifted when Mick Goodrick rejoined the faculty (after spending time on the faculty of New England Conservatory). I became acting chair in 1988, and chair in 1990. Rick came on in 1992 as assistant chair, and we hired Mick back about a year later. After that, Mick wanted to organize the materials—each semester would be different arpeggios, triads—and he instituted the fourth semester scales in the harmonic major. Upper semester voice-leading, three-octave scales—that came with Mick as well. He would bring these ideas to our faculty meetings, and we worked on it together: "How does this look?" And people said, "That's good, but..." So, it went on for a while like that, and then we said, "We're just going to do it. We can change the proficiency—it doesn't have to stay the same for thirty or forty years, it can be changed over time." But this one has lasted. This one works.

The following pages are intended as an introduction to the current Berklee College of Music guitar proficiency materials. These pages present one basic approach to each concept and data set included. Each day in the department, each of our more than fifty faculty members and hundreds of guitar students bring their own perspectives, variations, and applications to these materials, realizing them in their broad range of styles.

As you begin to learn them, you will bring these foundational materials to your own music.

Part I.
Proficiency Materials

CHAPTER 1

Super-Fundamentals

SUPER-FUNDAMENTALS: TECHNIQUE, TONE, NOTE LOCATION, RHYTHM

There are fundamentals at the root of all guitar playing. In the Berklee Guitar Department, Professor David Tronzo's term for this topic set is "super-fundamentals," because maximum progress on our instrument is only possible through practice and awareness of the way in which they work together.

These are:

- **Technique:** the way in which you physically approach your guitar

- **Tone Production:** your ability to control your sound

- **Note Location:** your ability to access the notes anywhere on your instrument

- **Rhythm:** your ability to play subdivisions of the beat, and demonstrate the basic feel of notes on the center of the beat, on the back of the beat, and on the front of the beat

TECHNIQUE

While the details and nuances of picking- and fretting-hand technique vary depending on your style, there are super-fundamentals common to us all. They include: breathing, posture, and picking- and fretting-hand positioning.

Breathing is the most fundamental of all techniques, and is the most-often overlooked. As we focus to practice difficult passages or push our speed and/or difficulty level, we tend to hold our breath. This constricts the blood flow from our torso to our shoulders, arms, and hands, and causes tension to creep into our hands and face. If we are unaware or inattentive to this tendency as we practice with repetition, the accompanying tension will imprint in our muscle memory. Playing with this tension results in a thin, constricted tone, inconsistent or rushed phrasing, and can lead to physical injury in the hands and shoulders. Learning to breathe while practicing literally "opens up" our bodies and our sound. When our body is breathing, our muscles relax, resulting in a full, open tone, fluid phrasing, and healthy hands.

As you play each example in this book, focus on your breathing as part of your technique. Begin playing by taking a few deep breaths before you play the first note. Pay attention to this feeling in your body. Play slowly, and as you play the example, be conscious that you continue to breathe as you are playing. As you increase your speed, or as you work on challenging examples, play short excerpts and take a deep breath between each repetition.

As your body imprints the physical act of breathing into your muscle memory, you are teaching yourself to breathe automatically as you perform. Listen to your tone as you breathe and play, becoming aware of the way your sound opens up as your body relaxes. Allow this tone and the accompanying breath to become a natural part of your guitar playing.

IN PRACTICE

Study 1. "The Breath, Qigong, and Musical Performance" by Joe Rogers, Assistant Professor

Posture

No matter our style of play, we all must position our bodies and our guitars in a relaxed, comfortable, and stable posture that supports both our picking and fretting hands. This creates the conditions necessary for a controlled sound and technical facility. Some guitarists play standing up with a guitar strap, others sitting down (with or without a strap), some sitting while positioning the instrument on the right leg, others with it positioned on the left. The authenticities of our styles inform these specific choices.

The following fundamental guidelines apply to all of us, regardless of style:

1. **Guitar Position.** The upper bout of the guitar's body should be central to your chest. This allows your shoulders to relax and remain level without hunching, and it allows both arms and hands to find their position comfortably. The height of the instrument may vary, with the breastbone being an important reference point. If the guitar is too low in the relationship to breastbone, the shoulders and wrists will strain as you reach down for the neck and strings. If the instrument is too high, the shoulders and arms will strain as you reach up.

2. **Fretting-Hand Position.** The general position of your fretting hand can be found by positioning your four fingers on the neck on one string, so that each finger gets a fret. The second and third fingers will be positioned "straight on," while the first finger leans toward the head of the guitar, and the fourth finger

leans toward the body of the guitar. The part of your hand at which the fingers meet the palm should be parallel to the guitar neck and slightly above the fingerboard. The fretting-hand wrist should be slightly curved outwards to align the hand—not bent in and concave. Your thumb's main job is balance, and, for this reason, it should rest on the back of the guitar neck (roughly between the first and second fingers) on its unbent tip joint. Some styles encourage the thumb to come over the top of the neck to occasionally fret a bass note on string ⑥. If this is true for you, remember that the most aligned position for your body has your thumb behind the neck; make this adjustment when those particular chord fingerings are not needed.

3. **Picking-Hand Position.** The basic picking-hand position can be found by draping your right arm across the body of the guitar on a diagonal. Whether you play with a pick or with your fingers, your pick and fingers will cross the strings diagonally. In addition to ease of crossing, playing the string on a diagonal creates a full, clear tone. If the angle is perpendicular, the tone will be thinner and brighter; parallel, the tone will be dark and can be muddy. There are three wrist motions that make a difference in the general picking-hand position: angle, height, and tilt. General alignment calls for no angle—a "straight wrist," in which your hand is aligned with your arm. For height, make sure the big knuckles of your hand are higher or at the same height as your wrist joint. In terms of tilt, notice that your arm and hand can rotate—as if you are turning a doorknob. Together, these three elements of alignment allow the hand to be supported by the arm and shoulder.

4. **Picking- and Fretting-Hand Coordination.** In each note played, your picking- and fretting-hand motions must be coordinated. If these motions are not in sync, your tone will be unclear and inconsistent. On a basic level, your fretting hand must lead your picking hand, securing the string before it is played by your pick or finger. Securing the string with a consistent contact point on the fretting-hand and picking-hand fingers while coordinating the playing motions is the key to producing a clear, consistent tone.

As you prepare each example in this book, be aware of your guitar position and the way your shoulders and arms feel as you touch your instrument. Check the position of your fretting and picking hands, ensuring that they are aligned. As you play each note, be aware of the timing of your fretting and picking hand—developing a physical sense of coordination and listening to the accompanying tone quality.

TONE PRODUCTION

The super-fundamentals of tone production are the parameters of sound, and the specific techniques required to produce them. Controlling these fundamentals requires the following: expressive intent, technical awareness, and a focused ear. (Remember that that super-fundamentals of posture are the foundation of these further developments.)

These include (but are not limited to):

1. **Dynamics.** Dynamics are controlled by the amount of weight placed on the

string by the picking-hand finger or the pick. The more weight placed on the string, the louder the dynamic.

2. **Attack.** Often confused with the technical approach to dynamics, the general approach to attack is controlled by the speed of your picking-hand follow-through (motion of your hand/finger) when playing the string. For a sharp attack, use a quick follow-through. For an open, round sound, use a slow follow-through. Another approach to attack considers the "envelope" of the note, referring to its shape and quality. Muted notes, slurs (hammer-ons/pull-offs), slides, staccato, legato, harmonics, all involve subtle differences in the attack and release of both the picking- and fretting-hand fingers to be played clearly.

3. **Timbre.** *Timbre* refers to the color of tone, and is controlled by the angle of the picking-hand finger or pick and by the placement of the picking hand relative to the bridge and the sound hole or pickups. Playing the string on a diagonal creates a full, clear tone. If the angle is perpendicular, the tone will be brighter; if the angle is more parallel, the tone will be darker. Positioning the picking hand close to the bridge produces the brightest sound; over the pickups or sound hole, the fullest; and close to the neck, the darkest.

As you play the examples in this book, be aware of your approach to tone production. Consciously choose a dynamic, an attack, and a color while playing, and work on the technical execution necessary to produce the parameters you have chosen. Remember: all of these expressive parameters are connected to your technique. Practice slowly, and allow your hands and ears to imprint these parameters into your muscle memory.

IN PRACTICE
Study 2. "Tone Study/Quartal Etude" (In A Melodic Minor) by Kim Perlak, Chair

NOTE LOCATION

The ability to locate notes across the fingerboard is another super-fundamental that is often overlooked. This ability can be constantly developed by recognizing, naming, and notating the notes in all of the examples to follow in this book. On a basic level, the following three approaches can be explored each day, using the natural notes in the musical alphabet.

1. **Notes on Each String.** If you are coming to this book with guitar experience, you know that the musical alphabet is made up of the notes: A, B, C, D, E, F, G. The notes of the musical alphabet are known as the "natural notes." These are notes that do not include sharps (♯) or flats (♭). The space between each note is called a step. There is a half step between the notes B and C and between E and F of the musical alphabet, and a whole step between every other pair of notes. On a single string, a half step is fret-to-fret, and a whole step is the distance of two

frets. Combine this knowledge with the names of the open strings on the guitar: ⑥=E, ⑤=A, ④=D, ③=G, ②=B, ①=E.

Starting with the first string, name the notes of the open string (E) and proceed up the string by step. Play only the natural notes of the musical alphabet, and memorize the fret number that corresponds with each note. As you become comfortable, improvise freely up and down the string, using only the natural notes. Move to each string in this method. Be sure to play past the 12th fret, naming and internalizing every possible fretted note on each string. Take the time to write out the notes on each string in notation on the staff.

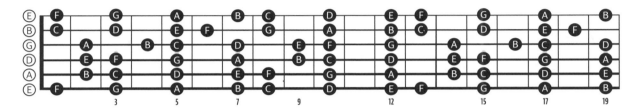

FIG. 1.1. Natural Notes on the Fretboard

2. **Notes in Position.** Notice that there are frets in which the natural notes occur across the strings with two one-note exceptions: on the open strings, and on frets 3, 5, 7, 10, 12, 15, 17, and 19. The exceptions to our natural-note consistency fall on frets 3, 7, 15, and 19, with a B♭ on string ③ fret 3; an F♯ on string ② fret 7, a B♭ on string ③ fret 15, and an F♯ on string ② fret 19.

- **Open Strings:**   ⑥=E   ⑤=A   ④=D   ③=G   ②=B   ①=E

- **3rd Fret:**   ⑥=G   ⑤=C   ④=F   ③=B♭   ②=D   ①=G

- **5th Fret:**   ⑥=A   ⑤=D   ④=G   ③=C   ②=E   ①=A

- **7th Fret:**   ⑥=B   ⑤=E   ④=A   ③=D   ②=F♯   ①=B

- **10th Fret:**   ⑥=D   ⑤=G   ④=C   ③=F   ②=A   ①=D

- **12th Fret:**   ⑥=E   ⑤=A   ④=D   ③=G   ②=B   ①=E

- **15th Fret:**   ⑥=G   ⑤=C   ④=F   ③=B♭   ②=D   ①=G

- **17th Fret:**   ⑥=A   ⑤=D   ④=G   ③=C   ②=E   ①=A

- **19th Fret:**   ⑥=B   ⑤=E   ④=A   ③=D   ②=F♯   ①=B

3. To work with playing the natural notes across the six strings with this approach, place the first finger of your fretting hand at each of these frets on string ⑥. When your first finger is at the 3rd fret, you'll be in the third position—notated as III. You'll play the natural notes of the musical alphabet as your fretting hand can stretch (a maximum of three notes per string), using the notes on the reference frets to guide you. Play across the strings, from ⑥ to ① and back again. Take care to avoid the sharp and flat, our two exceptions, in the reference frets! Adjust your fingering accordingly to play on natural notes. Play the natural

notes across the fretboard from each reference fret, naming and internalizing their locations. Take the time to write out the notes on each string in standard notation, in each position. Once you are comfortable, improvise freely across the strings, using only the natural notes.

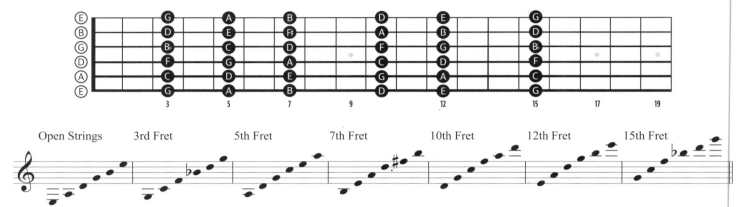

FIG. 1.2. Notes on Strings at the Reference Frets

4. **One Note on All Strings:** Now that you have secured the location of the natural notes, choose one note and play it in every location—in every octave—in every place it occurs on the fretboard. Once you have done this with one of the seven natural notes, repeat this exercise with each of the other six.

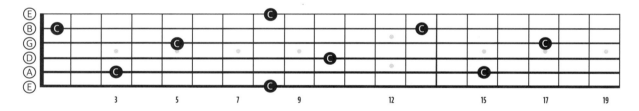

FIG. 1.3. One Note on All Strings: C

RHYTHM

The super-fundamentals of rhythm are your ability to demonstrate comfort with subdivisions of the beat, and the basic feel of playing (and hearing) the note on the center of the beat, on the back of the beat, and on the front of the beat. These are the fundamentals that can be applied to every groove and time feel required by the authenticity of your chosen style(s). In addition, your approach to rhythm affects your feel of the pulse, your phrasing, and your ability to create and interpret form.

To establish your super-fundamentals of rhythm, increase your ability to demonstrate the following:

1. **Subdivisions of the Beat:** Set your metronome to 60 bpm, and begin by thinking in 4/4 time and playing whole notes on the center of beat 1. Use your natural notes on the neck, in an area of your choice. Remember to incorporate the other super-fundamentals while playing! As you listen to and feel each note, internalize the duration of a whole note at this tempo. Repeat this exercise with half notes, and then with quarter notes. Next, turn your attention to subdivisions

of the beat. Play straight eighth notes: pay attention to your breathing as you play continuously. Next, play straight sixteenth notes continuously, stopping to breathe as necessary and being aware of your tone, attack, and timbre. Then combine the sixteenth-note subdivisions: first and second sixteenth notes, the second and third, the third and fourth. Keeping the metronome at 60 bpm, repeat this subdivision exercise with triplet subdivisions of the beat.

FIG. 1.4. Note Durations and Subdivisions

IN PRACTICE

Study 3. "Rhythmic Subdivision Workout" by David Tronzo, Professor
Study 4. "Introduction to Funk Guitar" (A Rhythm Study) by Jeffrey Lockhart, Professor

CHAPTER 2

Scales

THE MAJOR SCALE AND MODES

If you are coming to this book with musical experience, you will be familiar with the major scale: an arrangement of the musical alphabet that positions the half-steps between the third and fourth notes and the seventh and eighth notes. (The eighth note of the scale is the repeated first note one octave higher.) Sharps, which raise a note one half step, and flats, which lower a note one half step, are used in order to maintain the pattern in every key. For more information about the construction of major scales and their modes, please see *Berklee Music Theory*, by Paul Schmeling (Berklee Press, 2011).

In the proficiency, the modes are presented as "relative modes," meaning that they share the same notes as their parent scale and start on a different scale degree. *Ionian* starts on the first degree of the major scale, *Dorian* on the second, *Phrygian* on the third, *Lydian* on the fourth, *Mixolydian* on the fifth, *Aeolian* on the sixth, and *Locrian* on the seventh. The modes are identified by their start note in the parent scale and their modal name. For example, "C major from the fourth degree, F Lydian." Each mode is presented in its own two-octave fingering pattern, making seven patterns in total for each key.

These examples of the modes will be shown in the parent key of C major. You will notice that by practicing the super-fundamentals of note location across the strings in the previous section, you have already played several of the modal fingerings!

The first level of the proficiency requires demonstration of these seven major modes in the parent keys of C, F, B♭, E♭, G, D, and A. We encourage students to learn all seven patterns in all twelve keys. While there are different patterns used to play the modes on our instrument, the proficiency introduces these scales using common two-octave fingerings that use a maximum of three notes per string.

The following examples present the modes of the major scale in the parent key of C major, referencing both the start note in relationship to that parent key and the scale as a mode, with its modal name. Practice each of the modal patterns in the parent key of C major. Then, practice all seven modal patterns in all twelve keys. Practice writing out the notes of these patterns in standard notation as well as playing them on the instrument. When playing the modes, practice all of your super-fundamentals.

Mode 1.   C Major from the First Degree

C Ionian

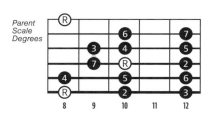

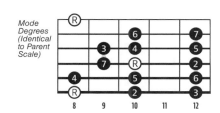

Mode 2.   C Major from the Second Degree

D Dorian

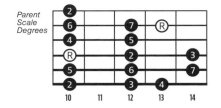

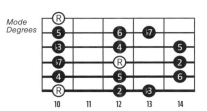

Mode 3.   C Major from the Third Degree

E Phrygian

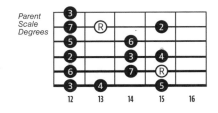

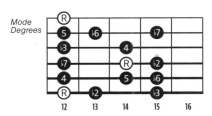

Mode 4.   C Major from the Fourth Degree   **F Lydian**

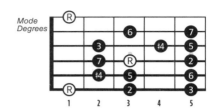

Mode 5.   C Major from the Fifth Degree   **G Mixolydian**

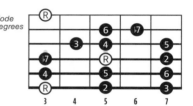

Mode 6.   C Major from the Sixth Degree   **A Aeolian**

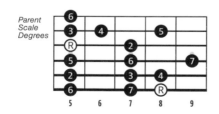

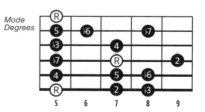

Mode 7.   C Major from the Seventh Degree   **B Locrian**

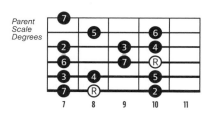

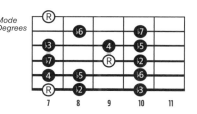

FIG. 2.1. Modes of C Major

IN PRACTICE

Study 6. "Modular Modes Study" by Abby Aronson Zocher, Professor

THE MELODIC MINOR SCALE AND MODES

The melodic minor scale used in the proficiency is also known as "jazz melodic minor." To create this scale, take the major scale and flat the third degree. Compared to the major scale, the numbered degrees of melodic minor are: 1 2 ♭3 4 5 6 7 1.

As before, these patterns are presented in common two-octave fingerings that use a maximum of three notes per string. Practice each of the modal patterns in the parent key of C melodic minor. Then, practice all seven modal patterns in all twelve keys. Practice writing out the notes of the patterns in standard notation as well as playing them on the instrument. When playing the modes, name them with the modal name and by the scale degree on which they begin. As you play, practice all of your super-fundamentals.

Mode 1.   C Melodic Minor from the First Degree   **C Melodic Minor**

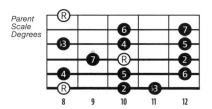

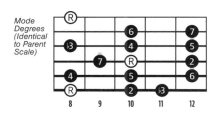

Mode 2.   C Melodic Minor
from the Second Degree

Dorian ♭2 or
Phrygian ♮6

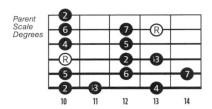

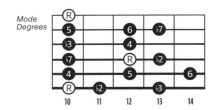

Mode 3.   C Melodic Minor
from the Third Degree

E♭ Lydian Augmented

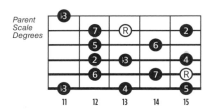

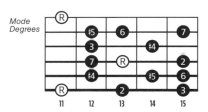

Mode 4.   C Melodic Minor
from the Fourth Degree

F Lydian ♭7 or
Mixolydian #4

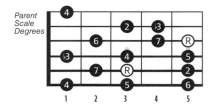

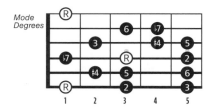

Mode 5. **C Melodic Minor**
from the Fifth Degree

G Mixolydian ♭6 or
Aeolian Major

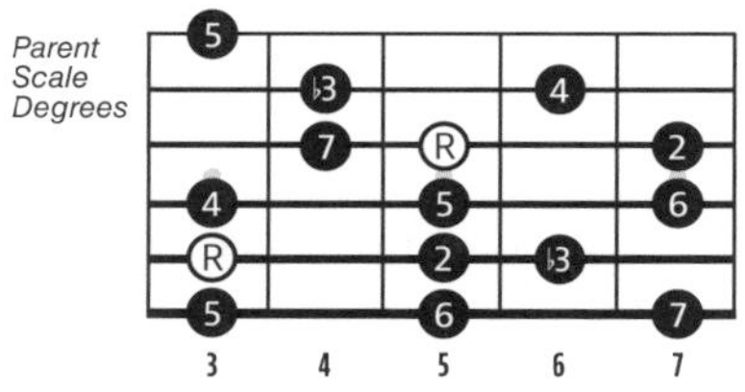

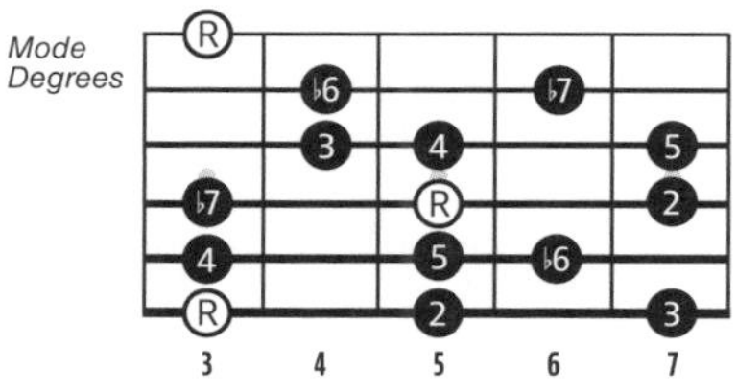

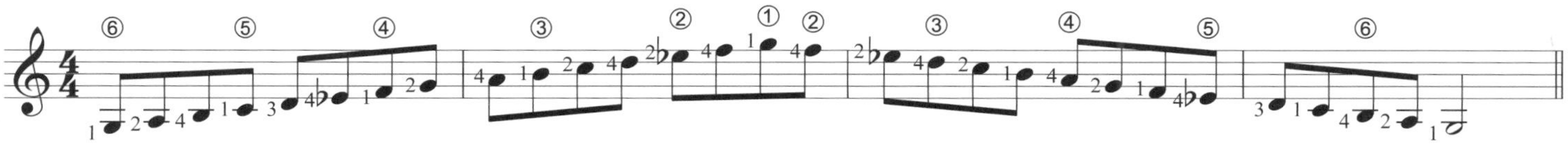

Mode 6. **C Melodic Minor**
from the Sixth Degree

Aeolian ♭5 or
A Locrian ♮2

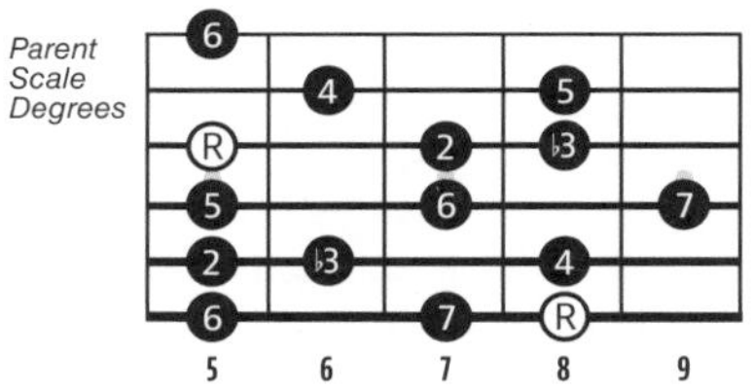

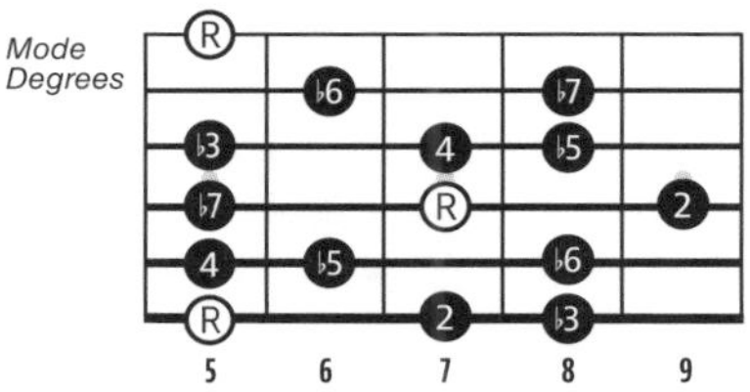

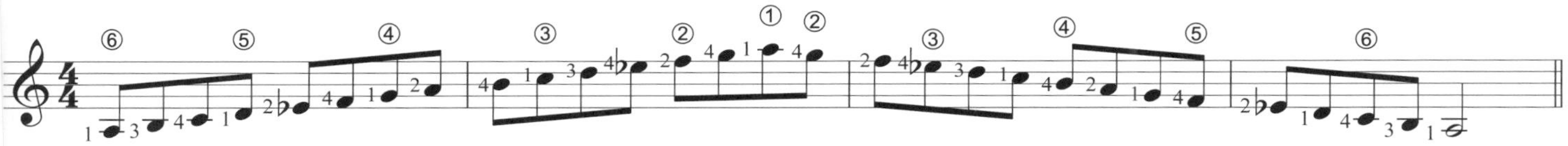

Mode 7. **C Melodic Minor**
from the Seventh Degree

B Altered or
Super Locrian

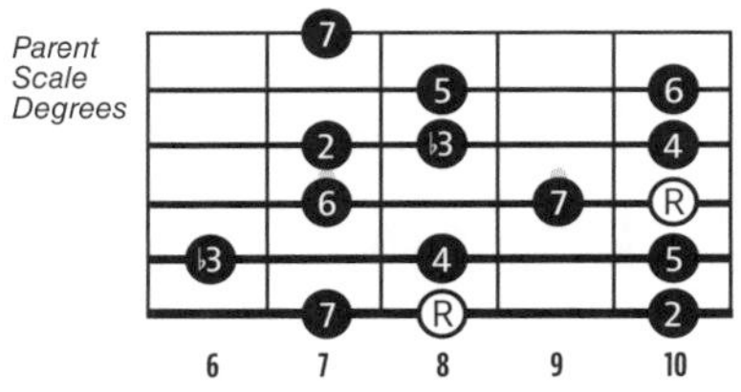

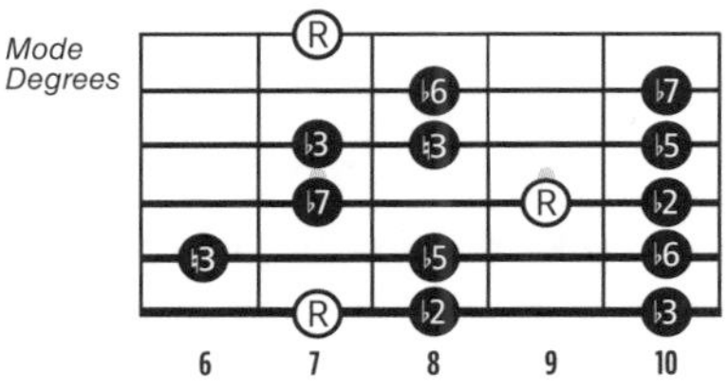

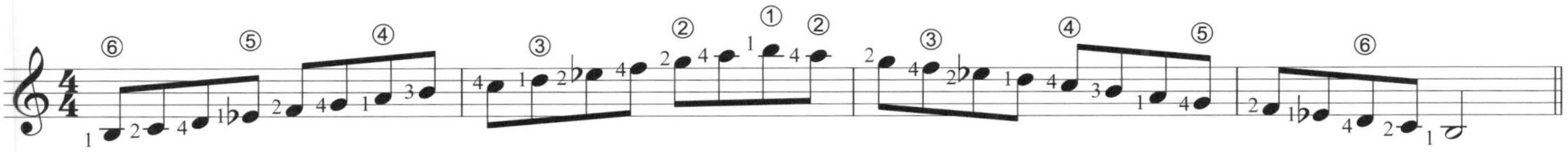

FIG. 2.2. Modes of C Melodic Minor

IN PRACTICE

Study 7. "C Minor Jazz/Blues, Melodic Minor" by Curt Shumate, Associate Professor

THE HARMONIC MINOR SCALE AND MODES

To build the harmonic minor scale, start with the melodic minor and flat its sixth degree. Compared to the major scale, the numbered degrees of harmonic minor are: 1 2 ♭3 4 5 ♭6 7 1.

As before, these patterns are presented in common two-octave fingerings that use a maximum of three notes per string. Practice each of the modal patterns in the parent key of C harmonic minor. Then, practice all seven modal patterns in all twelve keys. Practice writing out the notes of the scales as well as playing them on the instrument. When playing the modes, name them with the modal name and by the scale degree on which they begin. As you play, practice all of your super-fundamentals.

Mode 1.   **C Harmonic Minor from the First Degree**   **C Harmonic Minor**

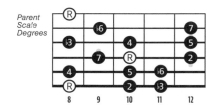
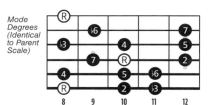

Mode 2.   **C Harmonic Minor from the Second Degree**   **D Locrian ♮6**

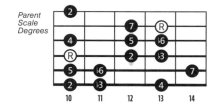
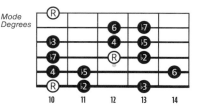

**Mode 3.   C Harmonic Minor
from the Third Degree**

E♭ Ionian #5

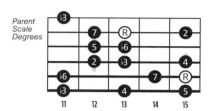

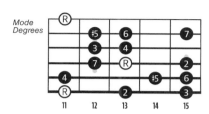

**Mode 4.   C Harmonic Minor
from the Fourth Degree**

F Dorian #4

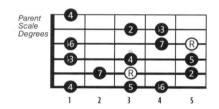

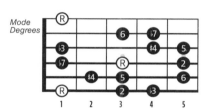

**Mode 5.   C Harmonic Minor
from the Fifth Degree**

**G Mixolydian ♭9, ♭13 or
Phrygian Major**

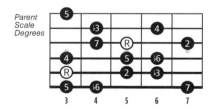

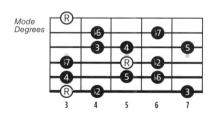

**Mode 6.   C Harmonic Minor
from the Sixth Degree**

**A♭ Lydian #9 or
A♭ Lydian #2**

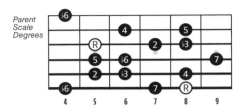

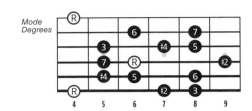

**Mode 7.   C Harmonic Minor
from the Seventh Degree**

**B Altered ♮6 or
B Altered Diminished 7**

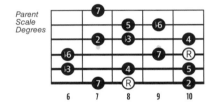

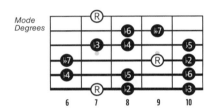

FIG. 2.3. Modes of C Harmonic Minor

IN PRACTICE

Study 8. "Transylvanian Requiem" (Harmonic Minor Etude) by Joe Stump, Professor

---

THE HARMONIC MAJOR SCALE AND MODES

To build the harmonic major scale, take the harmonic minor scale and raise the third degree by one half-step. Compared to the major scale, the numbered degrees of harmonic major are: 1 2 3 4 5 ♭6 7 1.

As before, these patterns are presented in common two-octave fingerings that use a maximum of three notes per string. Practice each of the modal patterns in the parent key of C harmonic major. Then, practice all seven modal patterns in all twelve keys. Practice writing out the notes of the scales as well as playing them on the instrument. When playing the modes, name them with the modal name and by the scale degree on which they begin. As you play, practice all of your super-fundamentals.

Mode 1.   C Harmonic Major
from the First Degree

C Harmonic Major

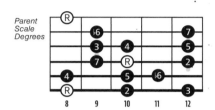

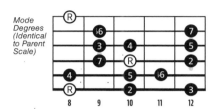

Mode 2.   C Harmonic Major
from the Second Degree

D Dorian ♭5

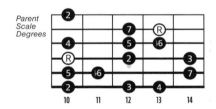

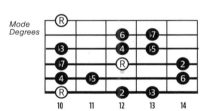

Mode 3.   C Harmonic Major
from the Third Degree

E Altered ♮5 or
Phrygian ♭4

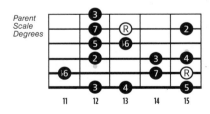

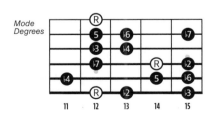

**Mode 4.   C Harmonic Major
from the Fourth Degree**

**F Melodic Minor ♯4 or
Lydian Diminished**

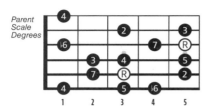

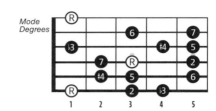

**Mode 5.   C Harmonic Major
from the Fifth Degree**

**G Mixolydian ♭9 or
G Mixolydian ♭2**

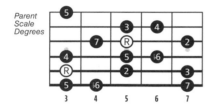

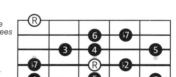

**Mode 6.   C Harmonic Major
from the Sixth Degree**

**A♭ Lydian Augmented ♯9 or
A♭ Lydian ♯2**

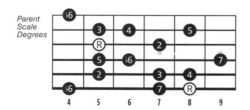

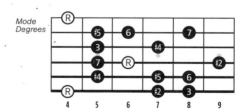

**Mode 7. C Harmonic Major
from the Seventh Degree**   **B Locrian Diminished 7**

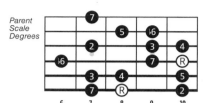

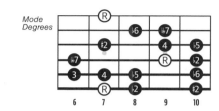

FIG. 2.4. Modes of C Harmonic Major

IN PRACTICE

Study 9. "Graffiti Cemetery" (Harmonic Major Groove) by David Fiuczynski, Professor

PRACTICING THE MODES

No matter your style, practice the seven modal fingerings in major, melodic minor, harmonic minor, and harmonic major, internalizing the scale degrees and the note names as you play them. Choose a parent key and one of the four scale types, and play all of the seven modal patterns. Next, choose one fingering pattern, and take it through the scale degree changes to create major, melodic minor, harmonic minor, and harmonic major.

The applications provided in chapter 7, "Studies," are a small collection of the possible stylistic applications of these modes. Though some may not be common in your current style, learning them will deepen your knowledge of the fingerboard. Use all of this material as a foundational starting point for your work in scales and modes on our instrument.

THREE-OCTAVE SCALES

At Berklee, levels 1–4 of the proficiency require two-octave patterns, such as those provided in this chapter. Levels 5–8 require three-octave fingering patterns for the modes, created by linking previous fingering patterns together. One common approach is to play four notes of the scale on each string, as in the following fingering for C major from the fourth degree (F Lydian). Looking at this example for reference, create three-octave patterns for major, melodic minor, harmonic minor, and harmonic major modes starting on each scale degree.

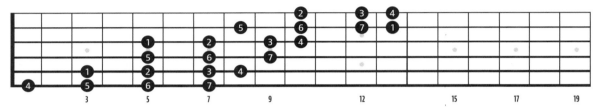

FIG. 2.5. C Major from the Fourth Degree, F Lydian in Three Octaves

SYMMETRICAL SCALES

Chromatic

The chromatic scale includes all twelve tones, each a half step apart. It is a symmetrical scale, meaning that the interval distance between each note is the same, and any note could be thought of as the tonic. There are different ways to play this scale across the fretboard. The fingering presented in the proficiency is a two-octave, moveable pattern that can begin on any note on string ⑥.

Figure 2.6 presents the chromatic scale starting on the note C. Practice this, and then move the pattern to start on different root notes. Once this fingering pattern feels comfortable, think of different fingerings you may use for the scale.

Notes of the chromatic scale, starting on C: C C♯ D D♯ E F F♯ G G♯ A A♯ B C

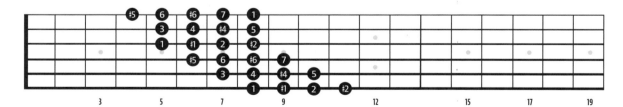

FIG. 2.6. C Chromatic Scale in Three Octaves

Whole Tone

The whole tone scale is symmetrical, meaning that all the notes are of equal distance—a whole step—apart. Each note of this six-note scale could be considered the tonic note because the equal distribution of intervals eliminates relative tension. There are really only two different whole tone scales. Starting on C, the notes would be:

- C D E F♯ G♯ A♯

- C♯ D♯ F G A B

The proficiency introduces two moveable fingerings for the whole tone scale to be played in two octaves-plus across all six strings, beginning on any fret. The following diagrams and notation present Whole Tone Scale 1 starting on C on string ⑥, and Whole Tone Scale 2 starting on C♯ on string ⑥.

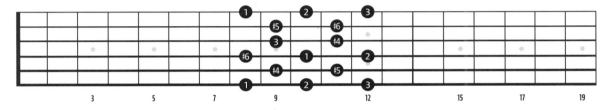

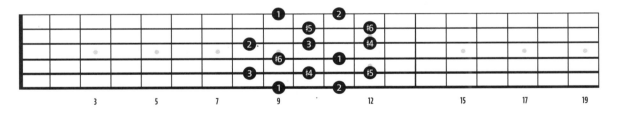

FIG. 2.7. Whole Tone Scale 1: Starting on C

FIG. 2.8. Whole Tone Scale 2: Starting on C♯

IN PRACTICE

Study 11. "Whole Lotta Whole Tone" (Whole Tone Scale Study) by Rick Peckham, Professor

Diminished

The diminished scale is an octatonic (eight-note) symmetrical scale consisting of alternating half steps and whole steps. Every other note outlines a diminished 7 chord. The proficiency introduces the most common fingering for this scale: a two-octave, moveable pattern that can begin on any note on string ⑥.

The following diagram and notation present the diminished scale starting on C.

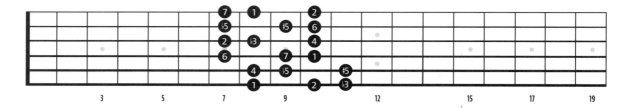

FIG. 2.9. C Diminished Scale in Two Octaves-Plus

IN PRACTICE

Study 12. "Diminished Scale Etude" by Rick Peckham, Professor

---

PENTATONIC SCALES

Pentatonic scales are five-note scales, and there are a few common types. Because the scale can be played on our instrument in five modes, with any of the five notes as the start-note, there are five common fingering patterns for each type of pentatonic. The proficiency introduces two types of pentatonic scales—the major pentatonic and the melodic minor "kumoi" pentatonic—and requires one fingering pattern/mode for each scale. Many guitarists are familiar with the minor pentatonic, which is commonly used in a variety of styles.

- The major pentatonic is scale degrees 1 2 3 5 6 from the major scale.
- The melodic minor pentatonic is scale degrees 1 2 ♭3 5 6 from the melodic minor scale.
- The minor pentatonic is scale degrees 1 ♭3 4 5 ♭7 from the natural minor scale (Aeolian mode).

The following diagrams and notation present one fingering for each common type of pentatonic scale in the first mode, beginning on C. Once you become familiar with each type of pentatonic scale, explore the fretboard to find and memorize the additional four modal fingerings for each type.

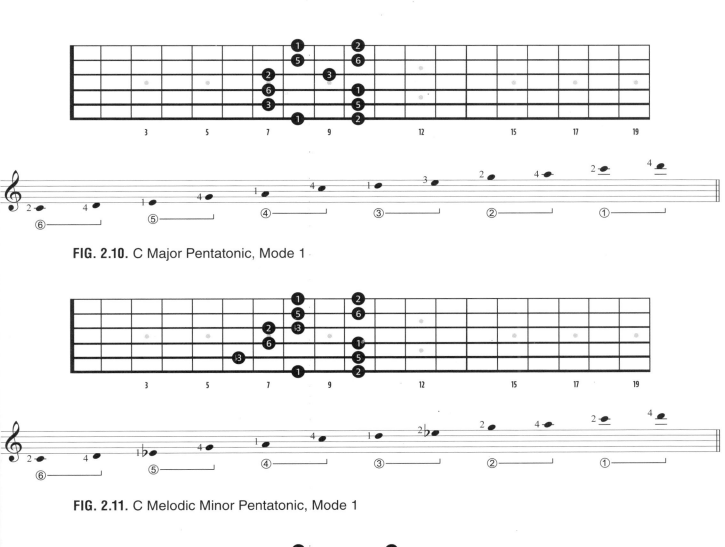

FIG. 2.10. C Major Pentatonic, Mode 1

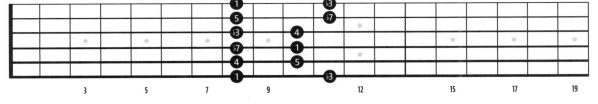

FIG. 2.11. C Melodic Minor Pentatonic, Mode 1

FIG. 2.12. C Minor Pentatonic, Mode 1

PRACTICING SCALES

All of these scales and modes will become part of your foundational vocabulary on our instrument. The practical and stylistic applications are so numerous that they will seem endless. Learn the fingerings and patterns in this section, internalizing the notation and scale-degree information as well as the pattern and its sound.

From this foundation, explore other fingering patterns for these scales and modes as well. For a comprehensive discussion and presentation of all scale fingerings in all keys, see *Berklee Guitar Scales* by Larry Baione (Berklee Press, 2018).

CHAPTER 3

Dyads

DYADS

Dyads, or intervals, are two-note structures. Dyads are used to imply harmony and to create counterpoint. Starting with the intervals of seconds through tenths, our faculty suggest learning each on all possible string sets—both isolating the interval, and then playing them diatonic to a major key. From here, practice the intervals in groups with their inversions and extensions, for example: seconds, sevenths, and ninths. Improvise with dyads, playing them together, and creating linear counterpoint by playing each note separately as you move from one to the next. Do this both diatonically and freely.

The fingerings for the dyads should be comfortable for your fretting hand. At different moments in your playing, you'll use the fingerings available as well as those you've internalized. To begin, consider that "each finger gets a fret," and the first and fourth fingers are the most natural to stretch.

Guitarists who have studied at Berklee may not recognize the topic of dyads as part of the proficiency final exam. Our faculty and chairs recognize the importance of dyads in developing an understanding of the way in which chords are built, and teach them as a prelude to triads and four-part chord forms and as tools to imply upper structures of complex harmony. For more information on the theory of building and naming intervals, understanding their inversions and extensions, and the term *diatonic*, please see *Berklee Music Theory* by Paul Schmeling.

ADJACENT-STRING DYADS

On adjacent strings, the minor-second fingering is the same for string pairs (⑥–⑤, ⑤–④, ④–③, and ②–①).

In the following diagrams, the lower note of the dyad is considered the root, and the upper note is named by scale degree in relationship to it. Please note that these intervals may be named or thought of with different scale degrees for both notes at times, depending on their use in a musical context.

Seconds: Minor and Major

The interval of a minor second is the distance of one half step.

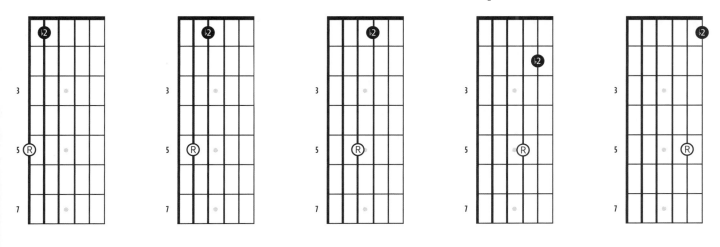

FIG. 3.1. Minor Seconds on Adjacent String Pairs

The interval of a major second is the distance of two half steps.

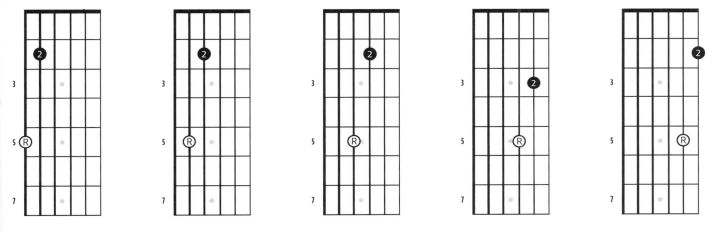

FIG. 3.2. Major Seconds on Adjacent String Pairs

In a major key, diatonic major seconds are built naturally on the first, second, fourth, fifth, and sixth degrees of the scale. Minor seconds are built naturally on the third and seventh scale degrees. Using the following notation and the dyad shapes you've memorized, play the diatonic seconds for C major in every place on the fretboard you can find them.

FIG. 3.3. Diatonic Seconds, C Major

Thirds: Minor and Major

The interval of a minor third is the distance of three half steps.

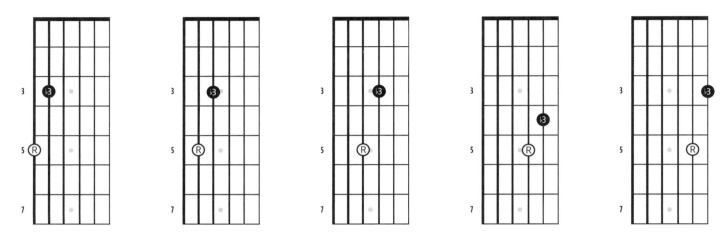

FIG. 3.4. Minor Thirds on Adjacent String Pairs

The interval of a major third is the distance of four half steps.

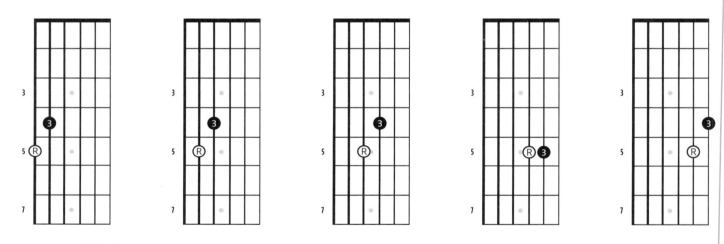

FIG. 3.5. Major Thirds on Adjacent String Pairs

In a major key, diatonic major thirds are built naturally on scale degrees 1, 4, and 5. Minor thirds are built naturally on scale degrees 2, 3, 6, and 7. Using the following notation and the dyad shapes you've memorized, play the diatonic thirds for C major in every place on the fretboard you can find them.

FIG. 3.6. Diatonic Thirds in C Major

Fourths: Perfect and Augmented

The interval of a perfect fourth is the distance of five half steps.

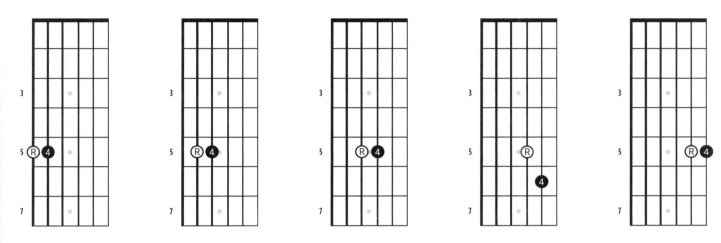

FIG. 3.7. Perfect Fourths on Adjacent String Pairs

The interval of an augmented fourth is the distance of six half steps. The enharmonic name for the augmented fourth—that is, the same interval distance of half steps from differently named pitches—is a *diminished fifth.* Another name for this interval is *tritone.*

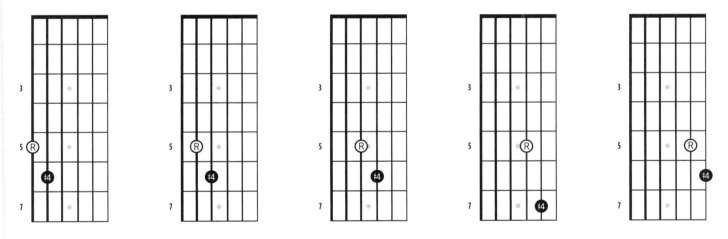

FIG. 3.8. Augmented Fourths/Diminished Fifths on Adjacent String Pairs

In a major key, diatonic perfect fourths are built naturally on scale degrees 1, 2, 3, 5, 6, and 7. An augmented fourth is built naturally on scale degree 4. Using the following notation and the dyad shapes you've memorized, play the diatonic fourths for C major in every place on the fretboard you can find them.

FIG. 3.9. Diatonic Fourths in C Major

Fifths: Perfect and Augmented

The interval of a perfect fifth is the distance of seven half steps.

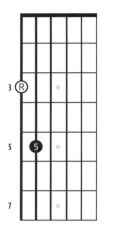 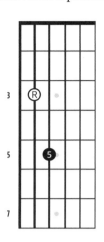 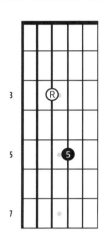 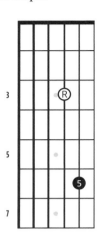 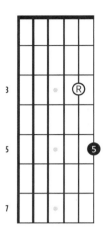

FIG. 3.10. Perfect Fifths on Adjacent String Pairs

The interval of an augmented fifth is the distance of eight half steps. The enharmonic equivalent of a augmented fifth is a *minor sixth*.

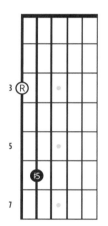 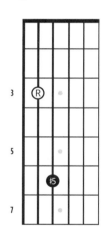 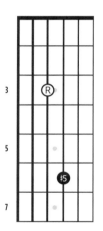 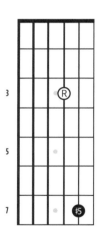 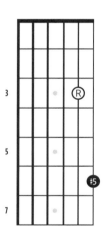

FIG. 3.11. Augmented Fifths/Minor Sixths on Adjacent String Pairs

In a major key, diatonic perfect fifths are built naturally on scale degrees 1, 2, 3, 4, 5, and 6. A diminished fifth (the same fingering as an *augmented fourth*) is built naturally on scale degree 7. Using the following notation and the dyad shapes you've memorized, play the diatonic fifths for C major in every place on the fretboard you can find them.

FIG. 3.12. Diatonic Fifths in C Major

ONE-STRING SKIP DYADS

For dyads played in a one-string skip fingering, the form is the same for the two string pairs ⑥–④ and ⑤–③, and the same for pairs ④–② and ③–①.

In the following diagrams, the lower note of the dyad is considered the root, and the upper note is named by scale degree in relationship to it. Please note that these intervals may be named or thought of with different scale degrees for both notes at times, depending on their use in a musical context.

Fifths: Perfect and Augmented

The interval of a perfect fifth is the distance of seven half steps.

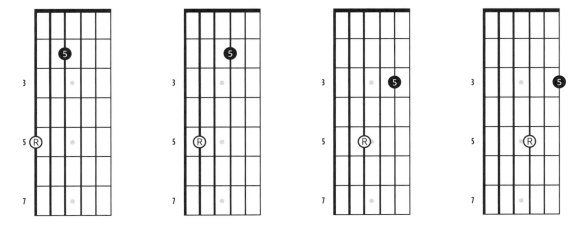

FIG. 3.13. Perfect Fifths, One-String Skip Pairs

The interval of an augmented fifth is the distance of eight half steps. For the diagrams of this fingering, see those of its enharmonic, the minor sixth, in the next section.

Sixths: Minor and Major

The interval of a minor sixth is the distance of eight half steps.

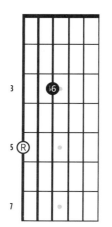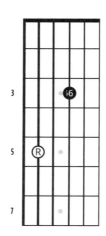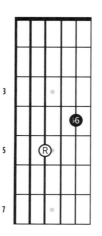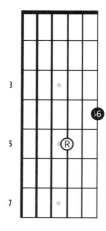

FIG. 3.14. Minor Sixths, One-String Skip Pairs

The interval of a major sixth is the distance of nine half steps.

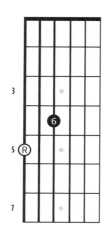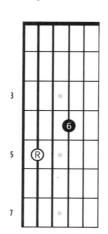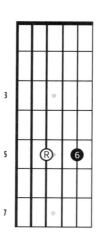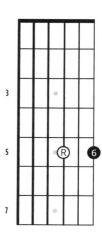

FIG. 3.15. Major Sixths, One-String Skip Pairs

In a major key, diatonic major sixths are built naturally on scale degrees 1, 2, 4, and 5. Minor sixths are built naturally on scale degrees 3, 6, and 7. Using the following notation and the dyad shapes you've memorized, play the diatonic sixths for C major in every place on the fretboard you can find them.

FIG. 3.16. Diatonic Sixths in C Major

Sevenths: Minor and Major

The interval of a minor seventh is the distance of ten half steps.

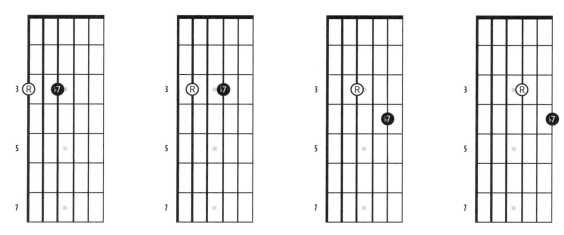

FIG. 3.17. Minor Sevenths, One-String Skip Pairs

The interval of a major seventh is the distance of eleven half steps.

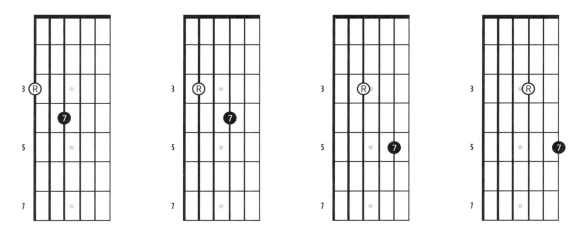

FIG. 3.18. Major Sevenths, One-String Skip Pairs

In a major key, diatonic major sevenths are built naturally on scale degrees 1 and 4. Minor sevenths are built naturally on scale degrees 2, 3, 5, 6, and 7. Using the following notation and the dyad shapes you've memorized, play the diatonic sevenths for C major in every place on the fretboard you can find them.

FIG. 3.19. Diatonic Sevenths in C Major

Octaves: Perfect

The interval of an octave is the distance of twelve half steps. In this interval, both notes bear the same note-name.

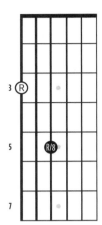 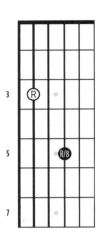 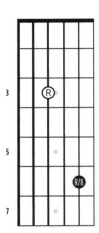 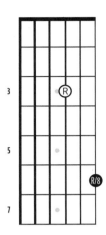

FIG. 3.20. Octaves, One-String Skip Pairs

In a major key, diatonic octaves are naturally perfect on all degrees of the scale. Using the following notation and the dyad shapes you've memorized, play the diatonic octaves for C major in every place on the fretboard you can find them.

FIG. 3.21. Diatonic Octaves in C Major

TWO-STRING SKIP DYADS

In a two-string skip dyad fingering, the fingering is the same for string-pairs ⑤–② and ④–①.

Ninths: Minor and Major

A minor ninth is a compound interval, built by combining an octave and a minor second.

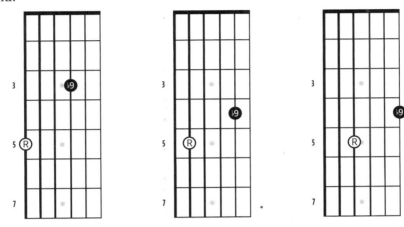

FIG. 3.22. Minor Ninths, Two-String Skip Pairs

A major ninth is a compound interval, built by combining an octave and a major second.

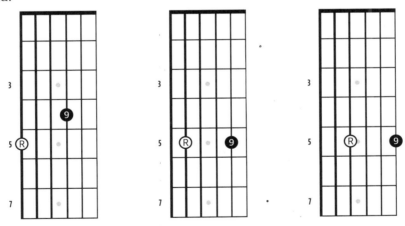

FIG. 3.23. Major Ninths, Two-String Skip Pairs

In a major key, diatonic ninths follow the same pattern as diatonic seconds. Using the following notation and the dyad shapes you've memorized, play the diatonic ninths for C major in every place on the fretboard you can find them.

FIG. 3.24. Diatonic Ninths in C Major

Tenths: Minor and Major

A minor tenth is a compound interval, built by combining an octave and a minor third.

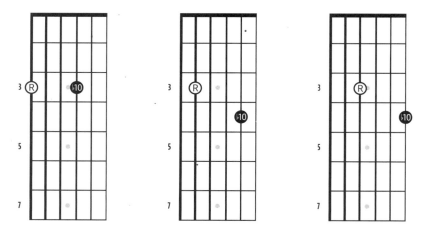

FIG. 3.25. Minor Tenths, Two-String Skip Pairs

A major tenth is a compound interval, built by combining an octave and a major third.

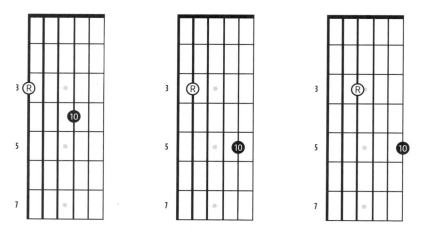

FIG. 3.26. Major Tenths, Two-String Skip Pairs

In a major key, diatonic tenths follow the same pattern as diatonic thirds. Using the following notation and the dyad shapes you've memorized, play the diatonic tenths for C major in every place on the fretboard you can find them.

FIG. 3.27. Diatonic Tenths in C Major

DYAD GROUPINGS

Dyads can be grouped and practiced together by choosing the smallest available interval, its inversion, and its compound interval. The inversion of a dyad can be found by taking the note on the higher string of the pair and dropping it one octave, or taking the note on the lower string of the pair and raising it one octave. Grouping the intervals in this manner allows us to hear the similar colors (*timbre*) of the close intervals, their inversions, and their extensions. Seconds, sevenths, and ninths can be grouped in this manner, as can thirds, sixths, and tenths. Fourths and fifths are paired as inversions, and often grouped together with octaves because of their timbre. Practice playing and listening to these groupings using the fingerings you've memorized.

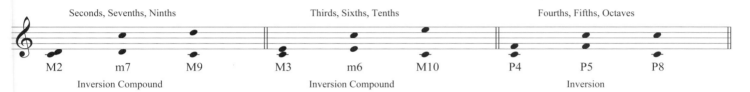

FIG. 3.28. Dyad Groupings

PRACTICING DYADS

In addition to playing the groupings, practice improvising with the dyads up and down string sets to create counterpoint. Begin with dyads on adjacent strings, and expand to the skip-string fingerings. Play the dyads together and displaced. Add a low-string bass note to your improvisation, and consider the possible chord tones you are creating with the dyads you choose. Experiment, and notate your ideas.

IN PRACTICE
Study 5. "Dyadic Etude" by David Tronzo, Professor

CHAPTER 4

Triads

TRIADS

A triad is a three-note chord form, built by stacking two intervals. The Berklee guitar proficiency focuses on voicings of tertiary triads—triads built with stacked thirds. The proficiency introduces fingerings for these chords on different string sets, close and spread; triad arpeggios, and voice-leading through triad *cycles*. In these voicings, the proficiencies require major, minor, diminished, and augmented triad qualities in all inversions.

- **Major triad** = a major third, with a minor third stacked on top of it.
- **Minor triad** = a minor third, with a major third stacked on top of it.
- **Diminished triad** = a minor third, with a minor third stacked on top of it.
- **Augmented triad** = a major third, with a major third stacked on top of it.

In each triad built in thirds, the interval between the root note and the top note is a type of fifth. In major and minor triads, the fifth is perfect. In diminished triads, this fifth is diminished. In augmented triads, this fifth is augmented.

If the notes are played in order: the root as the lowest, the third from the root as the second, and the fifth from the root as the top, the triad is in *root position*. If the third of the chord is on the bottom, the triad is in *first inversion*. If the fifth of the chord is in the bottom, the triad is in *second inversion*. For more information on the theory of building and naming tertiary triads, and understanding their inversions and extensions, please see *Berklee Music Theory* by Paul Schmeling.

FIG. 4.1. Triads in Root Position, First Inversion, and Second Inversion

The proficiency asks for a different way of voicing and practicing these triads in each leveled semester. Levels 1–4 require these triads to be played as chords across all six strings in close-voicing (on adjacent strings); up and down the string sets in close-voicing, starting from any inversion; in spread-voicings (on one or more non-adjacent strings), one-octave, starting from any inversion. Levels 1–4 require these triads to be played as one- and two-octave arpeggios, starting from any of the three chord tones. As with the modes, these levels include chords played from the following roots: C, F, B♭, E♭, G, D, and A.

Proficiency levels 5–8 ask that triads are voice-led through cycles, and extend the triad arpeggios to three octaves in all keys.

The following examples show each requirement from the root note of C. Begin with this, and then apply the fingerings and concepts to every root note. While practicing, be conscious of which scale degree is played by each finger, and the names of the notes you are playing. Take note of which scale degree is altered as you change from one triad quality to another.

CLOSE VOICING, ACROSS ONE OCTAVE

In a close-voicing triad, notes are played on three adjacent strings. Begin with the root position triad, voiced on strings ⑥–⑤–④. To find the first-inversion voicing on strings ⑤–④–③, raise the original root note one octave, moving it from string ⑥ to string ③. To find the second inversion voicing on strings ④–③–②, raise the third one octave, moving it from string ⑤ to string ②. To find the root position voicing on strings ③–②–①, raise the fifth one octave, moving it from string ④ to string ①.

For specific fingerings, think about your fretting hand. Play the fingering that feels comfortable to you, knowing that you may change fingerings depending on the musical context.

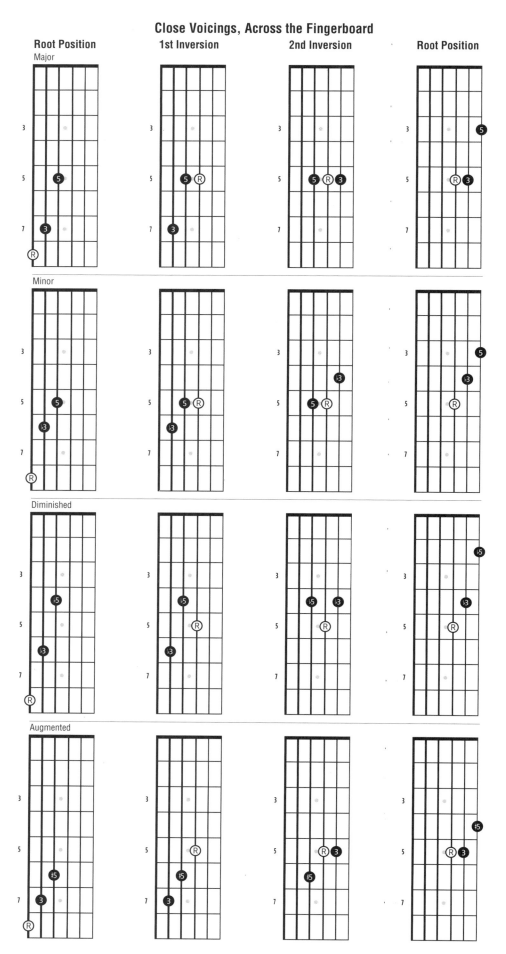

FIG. 4.2. Close Voicing, Across: Major, Minor, Diminished, Augmented

Close Voicing, "Up" and "Down" String Sets, One Octave

Now that you've played triad voicings across the strings, the proficiency invites you to move these triad voicings up and down a string set. Begin with the lowest possible inversion for the chosen chord and the string set. To move up the string set to the next inversion: move the root up to the third on the same string, move the third up to the fifth on the same string, and move the fifth up to the root. Repeat this process so that all inversions are played on each string set.

Major Triads "Up" All String Sets

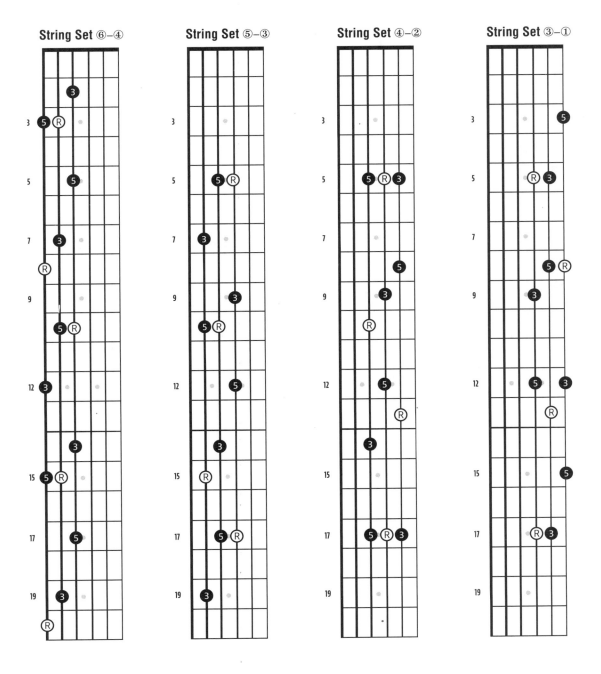

Minor Triads "Up" All String Sets

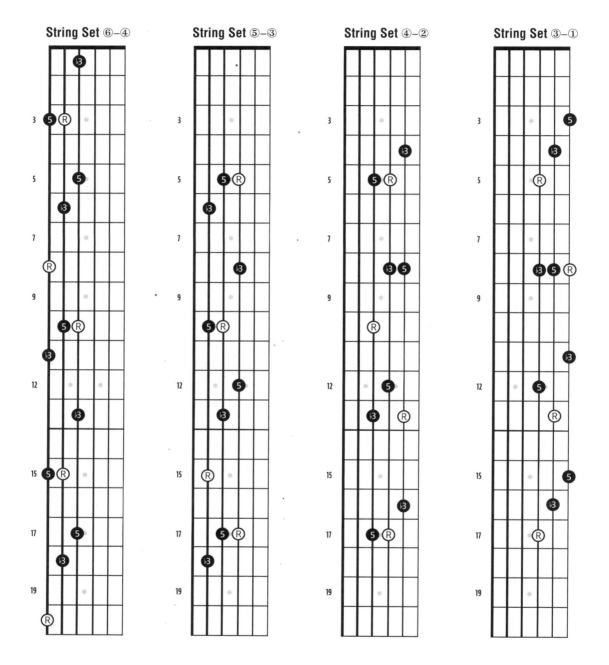

String Set ⑥–④   String Set ⑤–③   String Set ④–②   String Set ③–①

Diminished Triads "Up" All String Sets

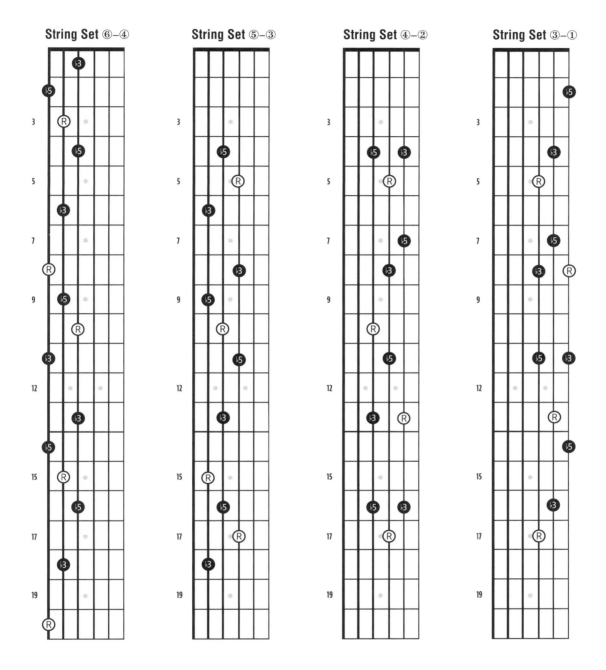

String Set ⑥–④   String Set ⑤–③   String Set ④–②   String Set ③–①

Augmented Triads "Up" All String Sets

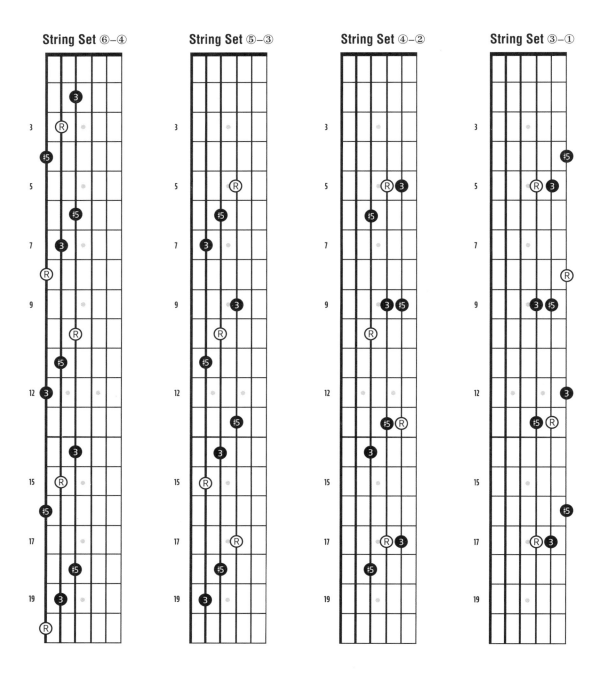

FIG. 4.3. Close-Voiced Triads "Up" Each String Set. In C: Major, Minor, Diminished, Augmented

IN PRACTICE

Study 13. "Close-Voiced Triads" by Jim Kelly, Professor

SPREAD-VOICED TRIADS

In spread-voiced triads, or "spread triads" at least two of the three notes of the triad are played on non-adjacent strings. Spread triads are created by starting with a close-voiced triad in any inversion, and raising or lowering the middle note by an octave. In spread triad-voicings, the triad is built as follows:

- Root position (low to high): Root, 5, 3
- First Inversion (low to high): 3, Root, 5
- Second Inversion (low to high); 5, 3, Root

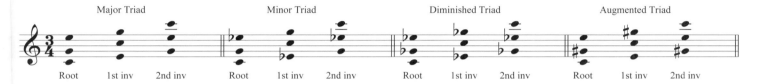

FIG. 4.4. Spread-Voiced Triads. In C: Major, Minor, Diminished, Augmented

To begin your work with spread triads, use these three fingerings: *upper adjacent*, in which the notes on the top two strings are played on adjacent strings; *lower adjacent*, in which the notes on the bottom two strings are played on adjacent strings; and *non-adjacent*, in which all of the notes are played on non-adjacent strings.

To practice taking one spread triad across the neck through each inversion, choose one of the inversions to play with its bass note on the ⑥ string. Move across the strings to the next fingering shape by moving "up" to the next string and using the next-highest chord tone as your bass note. Move the root up to the third, the third up to the fifth, and the fifth up to the root. As you change inversions, you will need to use all three different fingering types.

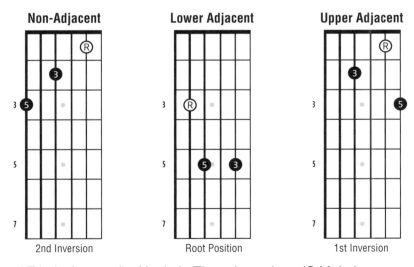

FIG. 4.5. Spread Triads Across the Neck, in Three Inversions (C Major)

Learn the progression of spread triad voicings across the strings in figure 4.5. Then, try this progression with different qualities of triads (minor, diminished, augmented). Experiment further on your own by choosing one of these voicings for one triad of your choice, and then looking for the closest notes available in a new triad moving across or up and down the guitar neck.

PRACTICING TRIADS

The most effective way to practice spread triads and close-voiced triads is by playing them in a piece of music. Take a chord progression from a piece of music you love, and find every way to play through it using close-voiced and spread triads. Triads can be thought of as vertical structures—as chords—and in a melodic way—to voice-lead counterpoint, and to create melodic lines. The triad cycles in the next section are an excellent way to practice voice-leading your triads. The triad arpeggios in the last section of the chapter will provide material to think of triads as melodic lines.

TRIAD CYCLES

The triad cycles were originally developed by Professor Mick Goodrick for his book, *Mr. Goodchord's Almanac of Guitar Voice-Leading for the Year 2001 and Beyond* (Liquid Harmony Publications, 2005). These cycles became an official part of the Berklee Guitar Department proficiency curriculum in 1992.

Levels 5–7 of the proficiency ask the player to voice lead triads through six cycles—chord progressions diatonic to the major, melodic minor, and harmonic minor scales. To be diatonic, the notes that build each triad on each scale degree must come from that particular scale. Level 8 asks that players voice lead any triad to any other triad, in a progression chosen by faculty adjudicators, in both close and spread voicings.

As you practice the cycles, it is helpful to know the basics of diatonic triadic harmony. Figure 4.6 shows the quality of each triad built on the scale degrees of three scales used in the proficiency cycles: major, melodic minor, and harmonic minor. For additional explanation of harmonic theory that will help you build on the following information, please see *The Berklee Book of Jazz Harmony*, by Joe Mulholland and Tom Hojnacki (Berklee Press, 2013).

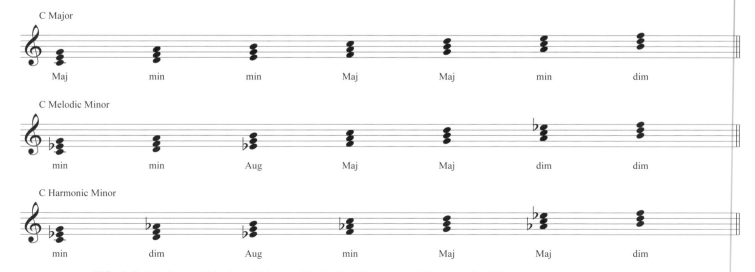

FIG. 4.6. Diatonic Triads of Major, Melodic Minor, and Harmonic Minor

The six cycles are identified by their original number in Mick's book, and with a direction (ascending or descending the fretboard) for the specific voice-leading. They are ordered here, and in the proficiency levels, by the number of common tones used in the voice-leading from chord to chord. The cycles can be started on any string set, and in any inversion. In order to complete the cycle using the indicated voice-leading, you will need all of the triad-inversion fingerings from earlier in this chapter.

To voice-lead from triad to triad, you will move each note of one chord to its closest chord tone in the next. For example, Cycle 3 is played descending and voice-led with two common tones. If the first triad, C major, is close-voiced on the string-set in the second inversion (③ = G, ② = C, ① = E), to voice-lead to the next triad, E minor, keep the common tones on strings ③ and ①, and drop the note on the second string by one half step: ③ = G, ② = B, ① = E.

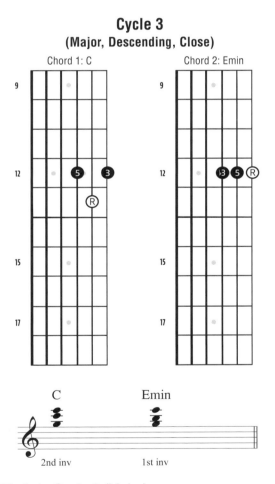

Cycle 3
(Major, Descending, Close)

FIG. 4.7. Voice-Leading Triads in Cycle 3 (Major)

The cycles are presented in this book as our faculty would ask you to practice these at Berklee: the specific fingerings for the triads in each cycle are for you to find for yourself! There is not just one option for each cycle!

To get you started, each major cycle that follows will include the first three possible triad voicings—close and spread. Begin with the examples, complete each cycle from this starting point, and apply this process to the cycles in melodic minor, harmonic minor, and harmonic major. As you explore the fingerboard and deepen your knowledge and comfort level with the locations of these voicings, begin each cycle on each possible string set, using close voicings, and starting the cycle with each possible inversion of the first chord. Repeat the same process beginning with each spread voicing of the first chord in each of its inversions.

MAJOR SCALE CHORD CYCLES

Cycle 3: Play Descending, Voice-Led with Two Common Tones

C Emin G Bdim Dmin F Amin C

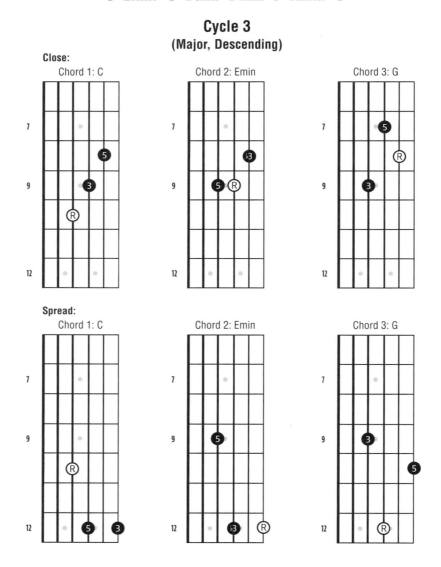

FIG. 4.8. Cycle 3, Major, First Three Voicings Option (a) Close (b) Spread

Cycle 6: Play Ascending, Voice-Led with Two Common Tones

C Amin F Dmin Bdim G Emin C

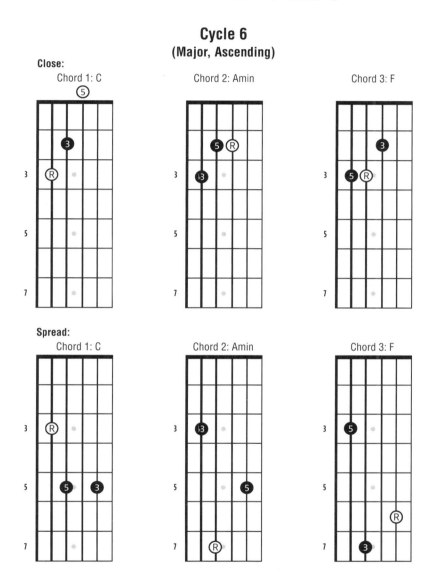

FIG. 4.9. Cycle 6 Major, First Three Voicings Option (a) Close (b) Spread

Cycle 5: Play Descending, Voice-Led with One Common Tone

C G Dmin Amin Emin Bdim F C

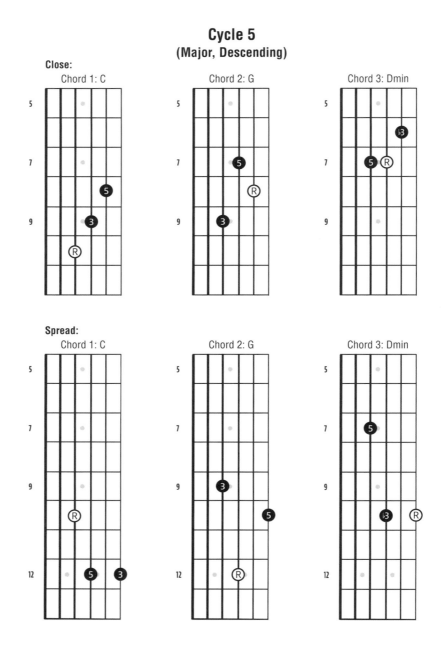

FIG. 4.10. Cycle 5, Major, First Three Voicing Options (a) Close (b) Spread

Cycle 4: Play Ascending, Voice-Led with One Common Tone

C F Bdim Emin Amin Dmin G C

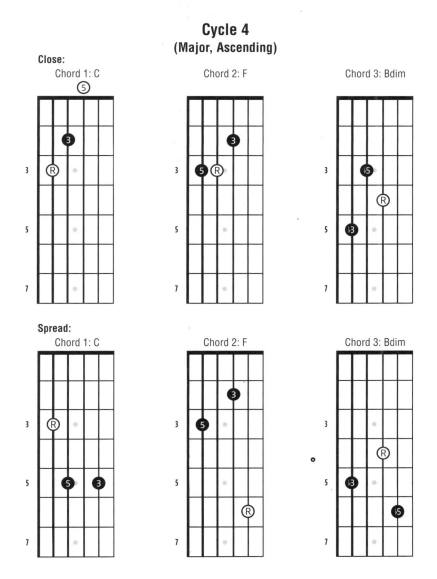

FIG. 4.11. Cycle 4, Major, First Three Voicings Options (a) Close (b) Spread

Cycle 2: Play Descending, or Parallel Ascending, Voice-Led with No Common Tones

If this cycle is played descending, each triad will be in a different inversion. If it is played ascending, each inversion will be the same for all triads, or *parallel ascending*.

C Dmin Emin F G Amin Bdim C

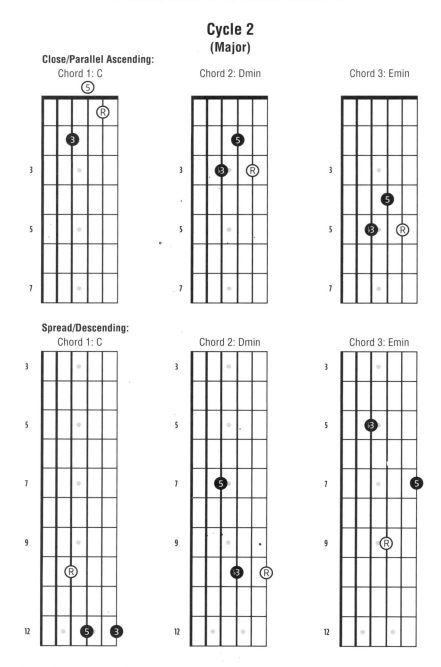

FIG. 4.12. Cycle 2, Major, First Three Voicing Options (a) Close (b) Spread

Cycle 7: Play Ascending or Parallel Descending, Voice-Led with No Common Tones

If this cycle is played ascending, each triad will be in a different inversion. If it is played descending, each inversion will be the same for all triads, or *parallel descending*.

C Bdim Amin G F Emin Dmin C

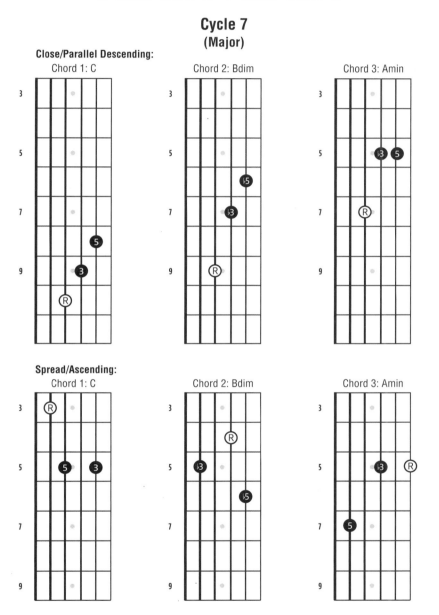

FIG. 4.13. Cycle 7, Major, First Three Voicing Options (a) Close (b) Spread

MELODIC MINOR SCALE CHORD CYCLES

Cycle 3: Play Descending, Voice-Led with Two Common Tones

Cmin Eb+ G Bdim Dmin F Adim Cmin

Cycle 6: Play Ascending, Voice-Led with Two Common Tones

Cmin Adim F Dmin Bdim G Eb+ Cmin

Cycle 5: Play Descending, Voice-Led with One Common Tone

Cmin G Dmin Adim Eb+ Bdim F Cmin

Cycle 4: Play Ascending, Voice-Led with One Common Tone

Cmin F Bdim Eb+ Adim Dmin G Cmin

Cycle 2: Play Descending, or Parallel Ascending, Voice-Led with No Common Tones

If this cycle is played descending, each triad will be in a different inversion. If it is played ascending, each inversion will be the same for all triads, or *parallel ascending.*

Cmin Dmin Eb+ F G Adim Bdim Cmin

Cycle 7: Play Ascending or Parallel Descending, Voice-Led with No Common Tones

If this cycle is played ascending, each triad will be in a different inversion. If it is played descending, each inversion will be the same for all triads, or *parallel descending.*

Cmin Bdim Adim G F Eb+ Dmin Cmin

HARMONIC MINOR SCALE CHORD CYCLES

Cycle 3: Play Descending, Voice-Led with Two Common Tones

Cmin Eb+ G Bdim Ddim Fmin Ab Cmin

Cycle 6: Play Ascending, Voice-Led with Two Common Tones

Cmin Ab Fmin Ddim Bdim G Eb+ C

Cycle 5: Play Descending, Voice-Led with One Common Tone

Cmin G Ddim Ab Eb+ Bdim Fmin Cmin

Cycle 4: Play Ascending, Voice-Led with One Common Tone

Cmin Fmin Bdim Eb+ Ab Ddim G Cmin

Cycle 2: Play Descending, or Parallel Ascending, Voice-Led with No Common Tones

If this cycle is played descending, each triad will be in a different inversion. If it is played ascending, each inversion will be the same for all triads, or *parallel ascending*.

Cmin Ddim Eb+ Fmin G Ab Bdim C

Cycle 7: Play Ascending or Parallel Descending, Voice-Led with No Common Tones

If this cycle is played ascending, each triad will be in a different inversion. If it is played descending, each inversion will be the same for all triads, or *parallel descending*.

Cmin Bdim Ab G Fmin Eb+ Ddim Cmin

TRIAD VOICE-LEADING "48 TO 48": ANY TRIAD VOICE-LED TO ANY OTHER TRIAD

4 Qualities x 12 Keys = 48 Triad Possibilities

Practice the following examples with both close and spread voicings, and create your own.

C Dmin E+ Fdim G Amin B+ Cdim D Emin F# G+ Adim B Cmin

C Abmin Bmin E A Ddim G+ F#min Bb Ebmin F Db E C

C Eb Gmin C E Db+ F Ebmin Bb F#min Eb+ Ddim A

TRIAD ARPEGGIOS

In a triad arpeggio, each note of the triad is played linearly—one after another—as if in a melodic line, allowing consecutive notes to be played on the same string as necessary.

Levels 1–4 ask for one- and two-octave arpeggios for all four triad qualities: major, minor, diminished, and augmented. Levels 5–8 ask for three-octave triad arpeggios. As in the scales and modes, the three-octave arpeggios combine the fingerings of more than one two-octave patterns.

TWO-OCTAVE ARPEGGIOS

The following examples show two-octave fingerings for each quality of triad, in each inversion. One-octave fingerings can be taken out of these patterns and practiced separately.

Triad Arpeggios
(Two Octaves)

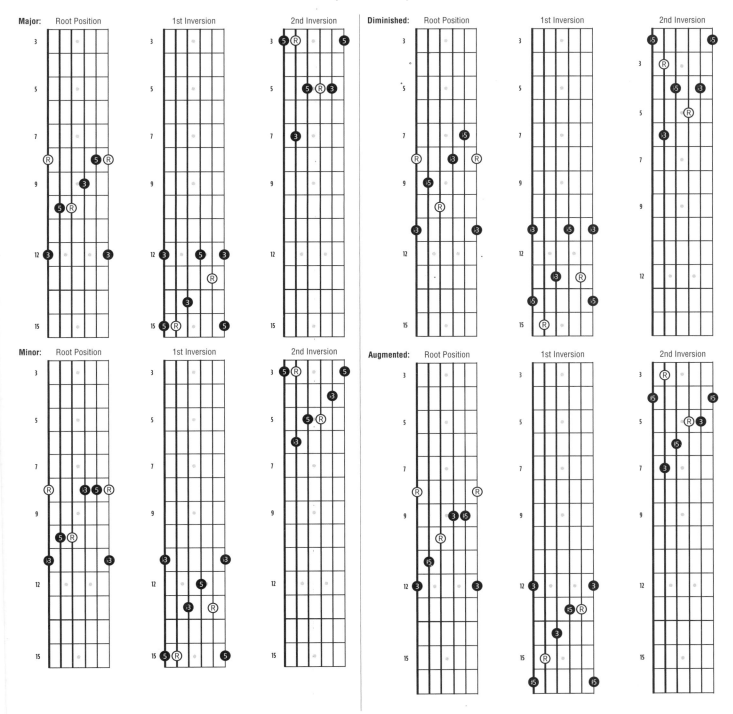

FIG. 4.14. Two-Octave Arpeggios: Major, Minor, Diminished, Augmented

IN PRACTICE

Study 14. "General Sense of Well-Being" (Fun Uses for Open-Voiced Arpeggios) by Jon Finn, Professor

Study 15. "Three-Octave Triad Arpeggios Strategies" by John Baboian, Professor

THREE-OCTAVE ARPEGGIOS

As with scales, three-octave arpeggios are created by linking the two-octave patterns and shifting between them. Our professor John Baboian developed a strategy for three-octave arpeggios that groups the strings in pairs as the arpeggio chain ascends. Take a look at figure 4.15 for an application of that strategy, and see the study from Professor John Baboian.

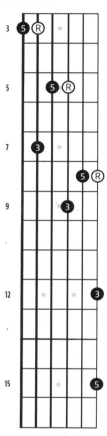

FIG. 4.15. Three-Octave Triad Arpeggio, C Major, 2nd Inversion

IN PRACTICE

Study 15. "Three-Octave Triad Arpeggios Strategies" by John Baboian, Professor

CHAPTER 5

Four-Part Chords

FOUR-PART CHORDS

The proficiency requires demonstration of four-part chords, focusing on seventh chords and voicings that contain extensions or suspensions. Levels 1–4 of the proficiency ask for twenty-six of these chords in two forms (fingerings) each, voiced in root position, with the roots played on both strings ⑥ and ⑤. As with modes and triads, the roots asked are: C, F, B♭, E♭, G, D, and A. Levels 5–8 ask for the same chords, in all keys, and to be played in all inversions. The fifty-two root-position forms are presented here in this chapter. These are meant to be a foundational starting point, learned with the understanding that players will continue on in their study of four-part voicings: in all inversions, with the root omitted, and in partial voicings.

The chord voicings included in this chapter can either be played diatonically in the modes of the major, melodic minor, harmonic minor, and harmonic major scales, or used as substitutions. The chords included here in Group 1 are built mainly with the major modes. Those in Group 2 are mainly built with the modes of the melodic minor, harmonic minor, and harmonic major scales. Knowing the basic diatonic function of seventh chords in each mode, and the way in which each chord included in the proficiency is built, will help you know how and when to use them in a stylistic context. Figure 5.1 presents the notation for diatonic harmonization of these modes, and the information that follows introduces the basics of chord-building. For additional explanation of harmonic theory that will help you build on the following information, please see *The Berklee Book of Jazz Harmony,* by Joe Mulholland and Tom Hojnacki.

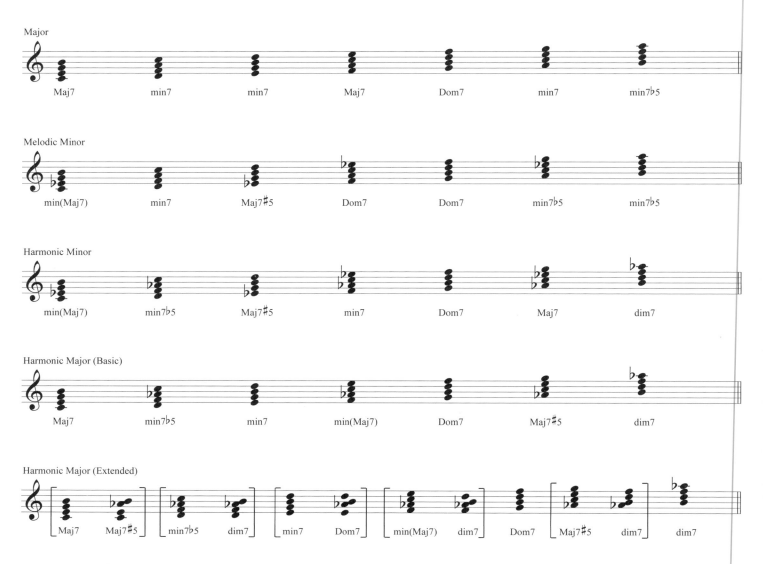

FIG. 5.1. Diatonic Seventh Chords for Major, Melodic Minor, Harmonic Minor, and Harmonic Major Scales

Seventh chords are built by stacking a diatonic third on top of a triad. The interval between the root of the chord and the top note is a type of seventh.

Maj7 chord = major triad with a major seventh (M7)

Dom7 chord, or 7 = a major triad with a minor seventh (♭7)

min7 chord = minor triad with a minor seventh (♭7)

min7♭5= diminished triad with a minor seventh (♭7)

dim 7, or °7 = diminished triad with a diminished seventh (♭♭7)

The following chords are alterations of seventh chords:

Dom7♭5 = dominant seventh chord, with a flat (or diminished) fifth (♭5)

Dom7♯5 = dominant seventh chord, with a raised (or augmented) fifth (♯5)

Maj7♯5 = major seventh chord, with a raised (or augmented) fifth (♯5)

Maj7♭5 = major seventh chord, with a flat (or diminished) fifth (♭5)

min7♯5 = minor seventh chord, with a raised (or augmented) fifth (♯5)

min/Maj7 = minor triad, with a major seventh (M7)

dim/Maj7 = diminished triad, with a major seventh (M7)

Dom7Sus4 chords replace the third of a Dom7 chord with the interval of a fourth from the root. **Sixth chords** add the interval of a sixth from the root note to a triad.

Dom7sus4 = play a dominant 7 chord, replacing the third of the chord with the fourth degree of the scale. The fourth degree is a suspension ("sus") in the chord.

Maj6 = major triad and a major sixth (M6)

min6 = minor triad and a major sixth (M6)

Ninth chords are extensions of seventh chords, built by stacking a third on top of a seventh chord. The top note is the interval of a ninth above the bass note. A major 9/6 chord adds a major ninth and a major sixth to a major triad. In a four-note voicing, players generally play the root, third, seventh, and ninth.

min9 = minor seventh chord, with a major ninth (M9)

Maj9/7 = major seventh chord, with a major ninth (M9)

Maj9/6 = major triad, with a major ninth and a major sixth (M6)

min9/Maj7 = minor ninth chord with a major seventh (M7)

Dom7(9) = dominant seventh chord, with a major ninth (M9)

Dom7(♭9) = dominant seventh chord, with a flat (or minor) ninth (♭9)

Dom7(♯9) = dominant seventh chord, with a raised (or augmented) ninth (♯9)

Thirteenth chords included here are extensions of a dominant seventh chord, with the interval of a thirteenth from the root added to the chord.

Dom7(♭9,♭13) = dominant seventh chord, with a flat (or minor) ninth (♭9) and a flat (or minor) thirteenth (♭13)

Dom7(♭9,13) = dominant seventh chord, with a flat (or minor) ninth (♭9) and a major thirteenth (M13).

Dom7(9,♭13) = dominant seventh chord, with a ninth (M9) and a flat (or minor) thirteenth (♭13)

Dom7(13) = dominant seventh chord with a major thirteenth (M13)

The fingering examples included here show two voicings of each chord in Group 1 and 2 in root position, with the root note of C. Note that some of these "four-part" voicings contain five notes: a voice that is doubled at the octave in a common fingering, or all of the extensions of the chord included. In the latter, you may decide to drop a note—depending on the musical context. The fingerings are presented here in two columns. Column 1 shows the voicing based on string ⑥, and Column 2 shows the voicing based on string ⑤. When practicing these four-part voicings, be conscious of the scale degrees you are playing with each finger. Identify the note name of each note you are playing in the fingering.

As you deepen your knowledge of the fingerboard, find fingerings for each chord in all inversions. Expanding your understanding of the notes and scale degrees you are playing will allow you to know when substitutions may be used in different contexts.

Group 1

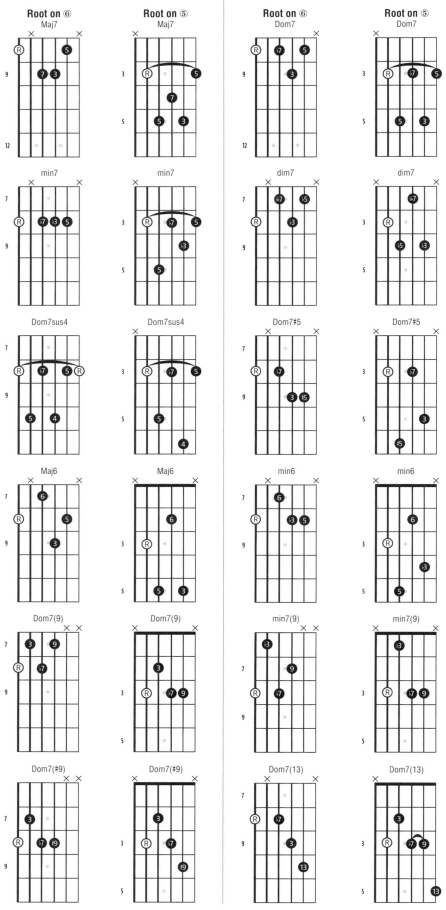

FIG. 5.2. Root Position Four-Part Chords, Group 1, Roots on ⑥ and ⑤

Group 2

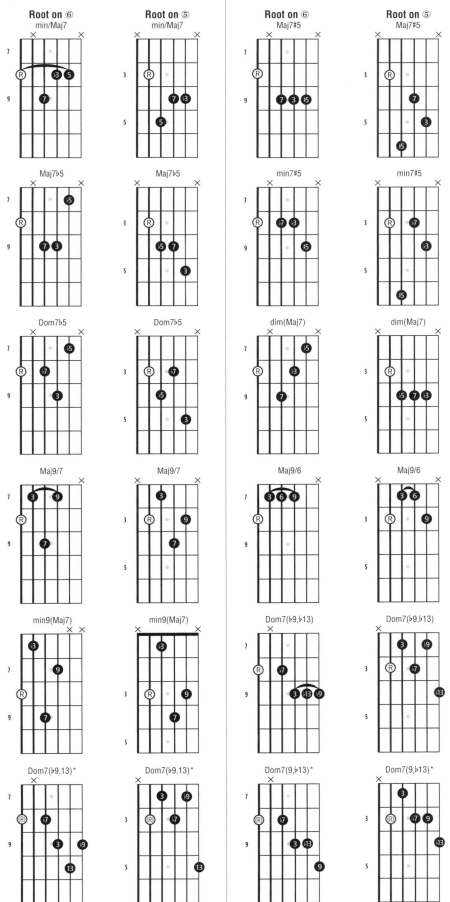

FIG. 5.3. 4-Part Chords, Group 2, Roots on ⑥ and ⑤. *For Dom7(♭9,13) and Dom7(9,♭13), omit the root for the most common four-part voicings.

Four-Part Chord Arpeggios

As with triads, in four-part chord arpeggios, each note of the triad is played linearly—one after another—as if in a melodic line, allowing consecutive notes to be played on the same string as necessary.

Levels 1–4 ask for one-octave arpeggios of a select group of seventh chords, starting from any note. As with modes, triads, and four-part chords, the keys asked are: C, F, B♭, E♭, G, D, A. Levels 5–8 ask for two- and three-octave arpeggios for this group of chords, from any note, in all keys.

As with the triads, learn the two-octave arpeggio fingerings here, and isolate one-octave fingerings from within these patterns. All of the four-part arpeggio diagrams that follow are presented in root position, from the note C. Learn these root-position arpeggios, and use your familiarity with the chord construction to derive and learn the inversions.

Two-Octave Four-Part Arpeggios

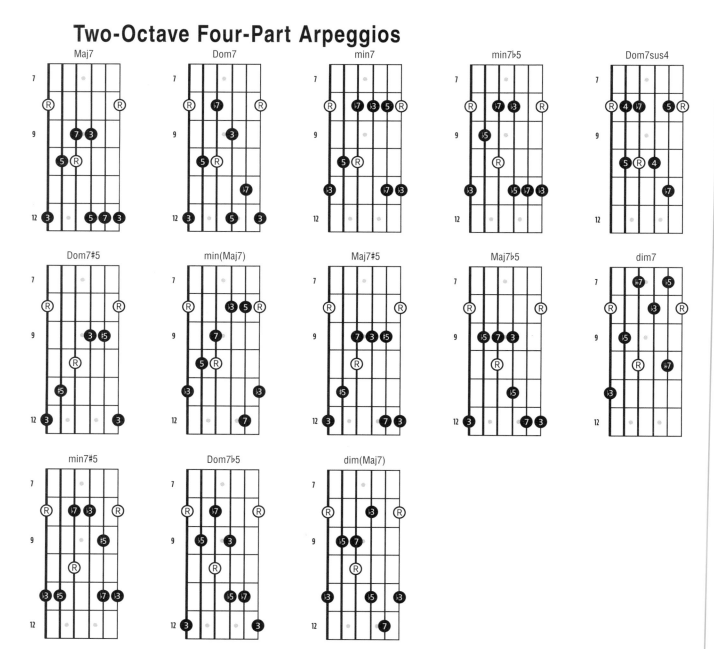

FIG. 5.4. Four-Part Arpeggios, Two Octaves, Root Position, from C

The four-part three-octave arpeggios are built by linking the patterns across the neck. Begin with the example included, and then create your own pathways through the fingerings. Figure 5.5 was arrived at using Professor John Baboian's strategy outlined in the triad arpeggio section of this book. Revisit this approach in his arpeggio lesson, included in chapter 7, "Studies."

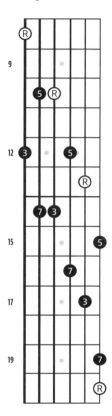

FIG. 5.5. Four-Part Arpeggio, Major, Three Octaves

PRACTICING FOUR-PART CHORDS AND ARPEGGIOS

The most effective way to practice four-part chords is with a piece of music. Part II of this book is a good place to start.

IN PRACTICE

Study 16. "Four-Part Chord Inversions Etude" by Larry Baione, Chair Emeritus
Study 17. "Melodic Etude" by Lauren Passarelli, Professor
Study 18. "Funky Albert" (Playing Dominant Seventh Arpeggios over the Blues) by Mike Williams, Professor

Part II.
Applications

CHAPTER 6

Reading

In the most recent addition to the proficiencies, professors Rick Peckham, Jim Kelly, and Mike Williams composed reading examples specifically designed to apply the concepts included in Levels 1–4 of the proficiencies. Students receive these charts two weeks in advance of the final exams, and prepare to play them as duos with one of the faculty adjudicators in their test.

The charts included here are past test examples for each of the first four levels. Practice each part, gathering materials from the chapters in this book to apply to each piece. Which scale fingerings might you choose to read and interpret the melody? To improvise with? Which dyads, triads, or four-part chords will you use? How will the super-fundamentals play a role?

LEVEL 1

Reading Exercise 1.1

Reading Exercise 1.2

Reading Exercise 1.3

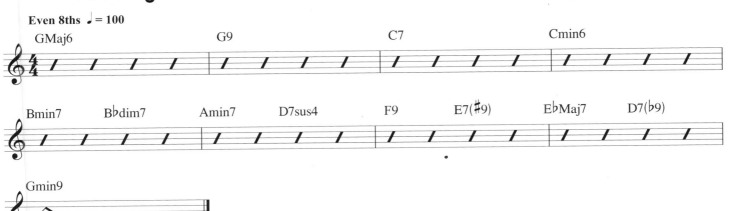

LEVEL 2
Reading Exercise 2.1

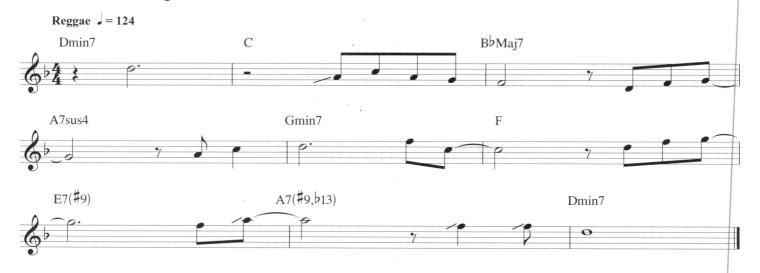

Reading Exercise 2.2

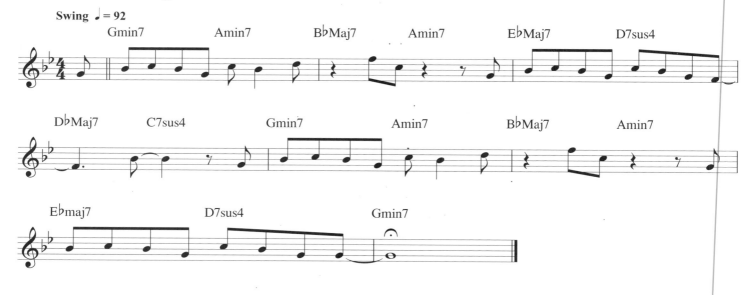

Reading Exercise 2.3

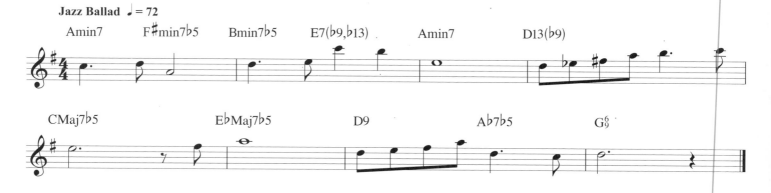

LEVEL 3

Reading Exercise 3.1

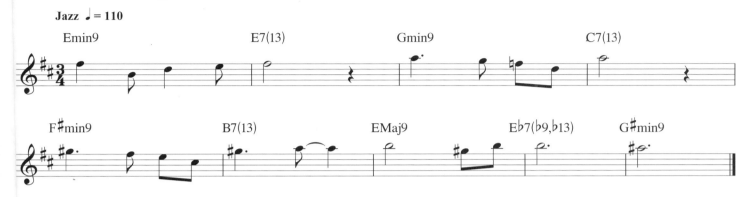

Reading Exercise 3.2

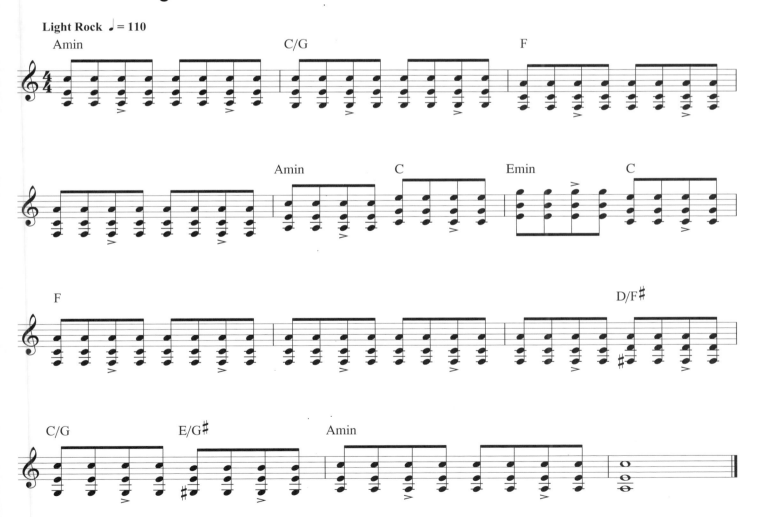

LEVEL 4

Reading Exercise 4.1

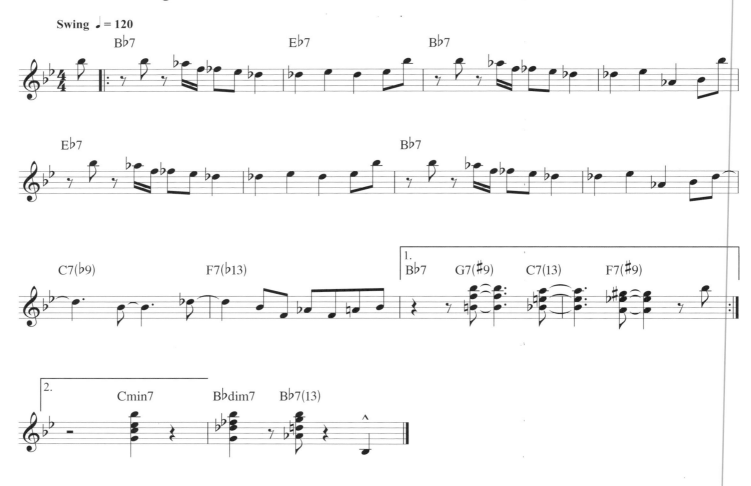

Reading Exercise 4.2

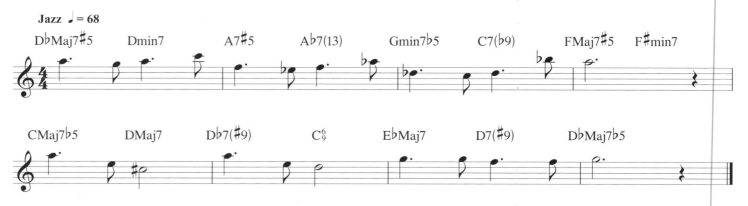

Reading Exercise 4.3

Note: The ⌐ articulations are played as (approximately) a ¼-step bend up.

CHAPTER 7

Studies

The techniques and concepts taught in our Berklee guitar curriculum, the super-fundamentals, and the proficiencies become a practical foundation for your creative playing, as they are internalized through intentional practice. The creative applications for these foundational materials are endless, and are present and possible in every style. The studies that follow, contributed by members of our full-time faculty, provide a small window into the range of possibilities that lie ahead for you in your playing.

STUDY 1. "THE BREATH, QIGONG, AND MUSICAL PERFORMANCE" BY JOE ROGERS, ASSISTANT PROFESSOR

As one approaches performance of a musical instrument, there is a certain sense of wonder, joy, and purpose which can elevate the performer above the normal state of consciousness. One's connection with their instrument can be a sacred communion. Here is a simple way to begin.

Find yourself in a comforting environment, free of distraction. In a seated posture, have your instrument resting before you. Take some deep breaths into your lower belly, expanding and contracting the abdomen with each inhalation and exhalation. As you are breathing in, imagine taking in creativity. As you are breathing out, expel any sense of limitation such as confusion or anxiousness.

You can be creative with this process. Be playful. You can try breathing in color. Start with red and work your way through the rainbow: red, orange, yellow, green, blue, indigo, and violet. Notice where in your body each color tends to get absorbed. As you exhale, notice as you start feeling fresher that your exhalations get clearer, longer, more even. Similarly, you may use different pitches and see where in your body are the resonant spaces for each. For example, does your heart resonate more with an F natural? Is an A natural causing your brow to get tingly? Explore!

Now that you are in a balanced, creative atmosphere, you are ready to pick up your instrument and play with the muse!

Sound and color are forms of energy, and can be used very successfully and skillfully as you learn to master the Art of Creativity. The Chinese word for the skillful practice of this energy is Qigong (pronounced *chee-gung*), the practice of which has been an endless source of inspiration for me and for millions of others.

STUDY 2. "TONE STUDY/QUARTAL ETUDE" (IN A MELODIC MINOR) BY KIM PERLAK, CHAIR

This contemplative etude was written in quartal harmony, meaning that each three-note chord is built with two stacked intervals of a fourth. These quartal triads harmonize a melody, which comes from the A melodic minor scale. In addition to being an interesting example of chords built by stacking dyads other than thirds, the harmonic color of this piece inspires work with tone production.

When learning this etude, go through the following steps:

1. Learn each phrase, finding a fingering that best brings out the timbre of the harmony. Incorporate open strings! What can you do with the placement of your picking hand to further bring out the timbre of each phrase?

2. As you internalize each phrase, consider your dynamics. Which dynamic is best for each phrase on its own? Within the context of the piece?

3. Consider the envelope of each chord: will you play them legato? Staccato? With a smooth or sharp attack? What about sustain and release? As part of your practice, play the top, middle, and bass notes of the chords in each phrase as separate melodic lines.

Practice the technique of your timbre, dynamics, and envelope so that you can execute what the music needs on demand.

Tone Study/Quartal Etude
In A Melodic Minor

Kim Perlak

Dark, Thoughtful, Connected ♩ = 54

STUDY 3. "RHYTHMIC SUBDIVISION WORKOUT" BY DAVID TRONZO, PROFESSOR

Included here are three rhythmic subdivision workouts (one in duple time, and two in triple), designed to promote familiarity and precision with various rhythms. Rhythmic diversity, understanding, and control are crucial, as rhythm is the first principle of music from which evolves all melody, harmony, form, and style.

The duple workout uses ten different sixteenth-note rhythms. The first triplet workout uses five different eighth-note triplet rhythms; the second is an eighth-note-to-quarter-note triplet conversion exercise. (Note that the syllables for triple time used here are: "1-trip-let." This is a common approach, as is the use of the syllables "1-la-li" as in chapter 1.)

1. With a metronome setting of 60 bpm, begin by counting aloud the full sixteenth-note or eighth-note triplet group syllables in time with each beat of the metronome. Keep counting the full group while tapping each rhythm example. When you are comfortable with the tapping exercise, move on to the playing exercise. Slow your metronome down to a manageable tempo. You can never practice too slowly!

2. Select a single mode of any scale type in any key, e.g., mode 3 of F major (F major from A), two octaves across all six strings. This is located between frets 5 and 8.

3. At the same metronome setting that you used in the tapping exercise, play the mode, using each rhythmic subdivision, one example at a time, ascending and descending for four to eight repetitions. Try to count aloud the full sixteenth-note or eighth-note triplet group syllables in time while you are playing any of the subdivision examples.

4. Now begin to improvise any note order in the mode while using the specific subdivision example. (Maintain correct mode fingerings while doing this!) Utilize rests of any duration, so long as you play the subdivision correctly when you resume improvising.

5. As you get more comfortable and accurate playing these subdivisions, begin to combine the exercises in pairs, trios, and more, until you can utilize all of the exercises in the set.

6. Next, you can combine all the exercises from the three sets and mix/match them to create a great variety of rhythmic diversity in your playing.

Any amount of work with these exercises will yield positive results in playing, hearing, reading, writing, and singing. Enjoy!

Sixteenth-Note Workout

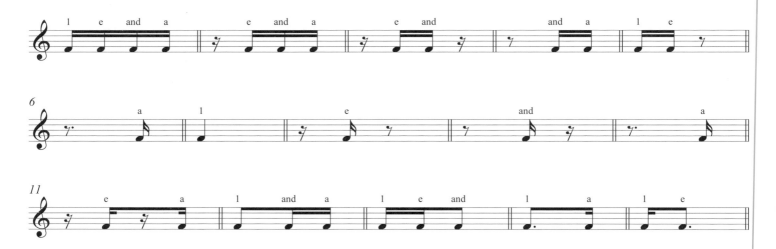

Triplet Workout 1

Triplet Workout 2

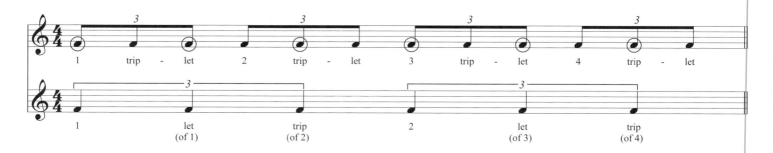

STUDY 4. "INTRODUCTION TO FUNK GUITAR" (A RHYTHM STUDY) BY JEFFREY LOCKHART, PROFESSOR

This is a funk guitar groove I created with different syncopated patterns. It is in 4/4 time. It should be played preferably with a drum beat. The purpose of this groove is to get you to play a repetitive pattern. The chord you will use is an E9. Try to lock into the guitar part and be consistent with it. You are just one part of the musical piece.

My approach to funk and groove is:

- Whatever it is you intend to play, play from the heart and soul.

- Funk is not always about 2 and 4, 1 and 3.

- The groove is in your soul.

I would like to help you find it.

Introduction to Funk Guitar
A Rhythm Study

Jeffrey Lockhart

STUDY 5. "DYADIC ETUDE" BY DAVID TRONZO, PROFESSOR

The dyads in this example create a rich melodic/harmonic progression and counterpoint with a minimal amount of pitches. The top voices form a melody that is in two parts, creating a question/answer form. The low voice melody is a counterpoint containing a descending whole tone line. The final statement of this low melody is an ascending line against a pedal point idea in the top voice.

Each melody can stand alone as a complete single voice statement. The dyads I selected focus in a specific harmonic content crucial to the mood or feeling of the piece.

I could, however, create multiple reharmonizations of the top voice melody by altering the low voice dyadic pairing. This is an interesting way to develop contrast while using the original melody before moving on to a new melodic idea.

An important equation to remember is: Content = Form, Form = Content.

It is important to learn all your dyadic interval fingerings, starting with minor/major seconds and continuing all the way up to compound minor/major sevenths (fourteenths!). You can harmonize melodies with great control and create a variety of harmonic and contrapuntal movement.

Dyadic Etude

David Tronzo

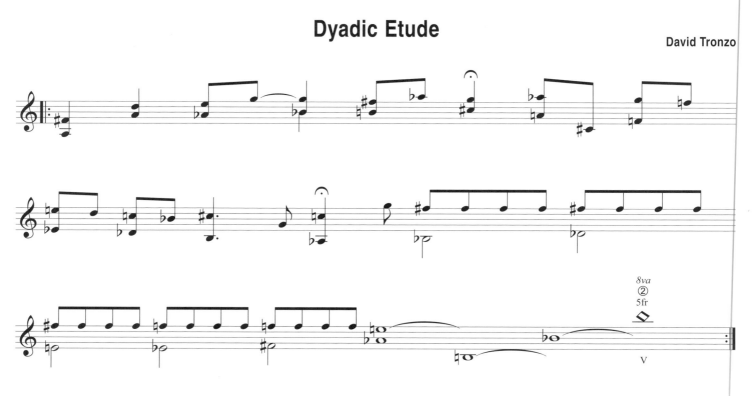

STUDY 6. "MODULAR MODES STUDY" BY ABBY ARONSON ZOCHER, PROFESSOR

This study uses the modes diatonic to C major, and is written in tribute to the great Mick Goodrick, titan of modern guitar and its pedagogy, and his "modal vamps."

This exercise is actually seven little exercises—or seven "mode modules"—that can be played individually, or put together in patterns. If you loop a two-measure mode module, this will help you play and hear that individual modal sound. When several modules are arranged in a particular combination, the resulting chord progression can sound one specific mode overall.

Once you learn to recognize modes and modal progressions, you will hear them all over the place! Identifying modal sounds in music is a wonderful trick, but that's just a fringe benefit; knowing the sounds of these modes and modal progressions is central to improvising, songwriting, and guitar playing in general.

Here are two ways to use this exercise:

1. Work on each mode separately, to learn the sound of each mode of the major scale, like this:

   Ionian mode:

   o   Learn the two-measure mode module marked C major (i.e., Ionian). Once you become comfortable with the marked fingerings and slurs, they will help the phrase sound and feel fluent.

   o   Loop the module by playing it repeatedly. (If you want to use an electronic looping device that's a great exercise too.)

   o   While the sound of the modal phrase is in your ear, play the diatonic chords derived from this mode: C major triad, and/or CMaj7. (You'll find the diatonic chords written above the staff.) You can do this by interspersing the chord into repetitions of the modal phrase, or by recording a backing track using those two chords and playing the phrase over the backing track.

   Dorian mode:

   o   Learn the two-measure mode module marked D Dorian.

   o   Loop the module.

   o   Play the diatonic chords derived from this mode (D minor triad, and/or Dmin7) during your looped modal phrase, or behind it by means of a backing track.

   Repeat the preceding process for each of the remaining modes.

2. **Play mode modules chained together to make a progression, using the following groupings.** Listen for the overall modal sound that results when that combination of modes is grouped that way. You can also record and loop the chain of modules, and then accompany it with the corresponding chords.

     o   **C Ionian (C Major) Progression:**

C Ionian module → F Lydian module → G Mixolydian module → C Ionian module

Note: When you play those modules in that order, you will effectively be "sounding" this progression: CMaj7, FMaj7, G7, CMaj7 (or a I, IV, V, I in C), and you will be creating the overall sound of C Ionian (C major).

     o   **D Dorian Progression:**

D Dorian module → G Mixolydian module (repeat)

Progression Sounded: Dmin7, G7 (or a Imin7, IV7 in D)
Overall Sound: D Dorian. For more examples of progressions that "sound" Dorian mode, listen to "Oye Como Va" by Tito Puente/Carlos Santana, or "Breathe" by Pink Floyd.

     o   **E Phrygian Progression:**

E Phrygian module → F Lydian module (repeat)

Progression Sounded: Emin, F major (or a Imin, bII major)
Overall Sound: E Phrygian. For more examples of progressions that "sound" Phrygian mode, listen to "Go Ask Alice" by Jefferson Airplane, or the opening phrase of "Wherever I May Roam" by Metallica.

     o   **F Lydian Progression:**

F Lydian module → G Mixolydian module (repeat)

Progression sounded: F major, G major (or I major, II major in F)
Overall sound: F Lydian. For more examples of progressions that "sound" Lydian mode, listen to the opening sections of "Here Comes My Girl" by Tom Petty, or "Sara" by Fleetwood Mac. If you add 7's to these triads, make sure you use the 7's diatonic to C major, which would be FMaj7 and G7; i.e., don't use an F7 or GMaj7, as those are not from C major, and so belong in a different exercise ☺.

     o   **G Mixolydian Progression:**

G Mixolydian module → F Lydian module (repeat)

Progression Sounded: G major, F major (or I major, bVII major in G)
Overall Sound: G Mixolydian. For more examples of progressions that "sound" Mixolydian mode, listen to "Fire on the Mountain" by the Grateful Dead, or "Tequila" by Chuck Rio, recorded by the Champs. (If you add 7's to these triads, make sure you use G7 and FMaj7).

○   **A Aeolian Progression:**

A Aeolian module → G Mixolydian module → F Lydian module → G Mixolydian module

Progression sounded: Amin, G major, F major, G major (or Imin, ♭VII major, ♭VI major in A)

Overall Sound: A Aeolian. For more examples of progressions that "sound" Aeolian mode, listen to "Stairway to Heaven" by Led Zeppelin, or "All Along the Watchtower" by Jimi Hendrix. (If you add 7's to these triads, make sure you use FMaj7 and G7).

Notation: Left hand = 1, 2, 3, 4. Right hand: *p* = thumb, *i* = index, *m* = middle, *a* = ring finger

Module 1: Ionian

Scale/Mode: C Ionian (C major from the root)

Chords derived: C major triad, CMaj7 chord (harmonic function in C major: I major, IMaj7)

Module 2: Dorian

Scale/Mode: D Dorian (C major from the 2nd degree)

Chords derived: D minor triad, Dmin7 chord (harmonic function in C major: II minor, IImin7)

Module 3: Phrygian

Scale/Mode: D Phrygian (C major from the 3rd degree)

Chords derived: E minor triad, Emin7 chord (harmonic function in C major: III minor, IIImin7)

Module 4: Lydian

Scale/Mode: F Lydian (C major from the 4th degree)

Chords derived: F major triad, FMaj7 chord (harmonic function in C major: IV major, IVMaj7)

Module 5: Mixolydian

Scale/Mode: G Mixolydian (C major from the 5th degree)

Chords derived: G major triad, G7 chord (harmonic function in C major: V7)

Module 6: Aeolian

Scale/Mode: A Aeolian (C major from the 6th degree)

Chords derived: A minor triad, Amin7 chord (harmonic function in C major: VImin, VImin7)

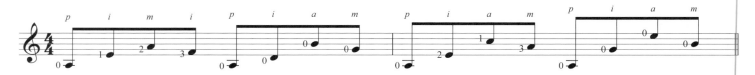

Module 7: Locrian

Scale/Mode: B Locrian (C major from the 7th degree)

Chords derived: B diminished triad, Bmin7♭5 chord (harmonic function in C major: VIIdim, VIImin7♭5)

STUDY 7. "C MINOR JAZZ/BLUES, MELODIC MINOR" BY CURT SHUMATE, ASSOCIATE PROFESSOR

The minor jazz/blues is a form that contains many possibilities for uses of the melodic minor scale and its modes. This three-chorus solo uses scale patterns as well as triads and seventh-chord arpeggios chosen from the corresponding melodic minor scales.

Chorus 1

The solo starts by establishing the blues tonality in the first couple of bars. However, by bar 4, the altered scale (seventh mode of melodic minor) can be used on the C7alt chord to create tension resolving into the IVmin7 in bar 5. Likewise, in bar 6, the G altered scale can be used to create tension resolving back to the Imin7 chord. The Amin7b5 is imposed on bar 8 (an inversion of Cmin6). The sixth mode, Locrian natural 9, is used here. The next two chords are typical of minor blues: bVI7 (sub V of V) and V7alt. The Ab7 accepts the fourth mode (Lydian b7), and the V7alt accepts the altered scale. The notes here are derived from each chord scale respectively.

Chorus 2

The second chorus starts off with a figure commonly used by such players as Wes Montgomery: using the relative Maj7 chord arpeggio on a minor tonality (e.g., EbMaj7 arpeggio over Cmin7). Bar 4 of the second chorus (bar 16 on chart) again uses the altered scale, this time almost spelling the Dbmin(Maj7) chord arpeggio. Bar 16, the second bar of the IVmin7 chord, again imposes the G7 altered scale to create tension resolving back to Cmin7. The next bar contains a Dmin7b5 arpeggio against the Ab13. This chord is chosen from the diatonic VIImin7b5 chord of the relative Eb melodic minor scale. The next bar contains two adjacent triads: bIII+ and IV major from the relative Ab melodic minor scale.

Chorus 3

The third chorus starts with a continuation of the major 7 interval used in the last bar of chorus 2. The major 7 interval is a strong sound used by Thelonious Monk and guitarists Joe Pass, John Scofield, and many others. This motive is developed through the first few bars of chorus 3, finishing with the major 7 interval on the C7alt chord (taken from Db melodic minor). The C7alt chord again uses a Dbmin(Maj7) chord arpeggio to resolve strongly into IVmin7. The next two bars use a similar motive, with chromaticism. The second uses an augmented Maj7 arpeggio over the imposed G7alt chord, resolving back to Imin7. The turnaround chords (bars 33 and 34) again use adjacent triad pairs from the corresponding melodic minor scales (Cdim and Ddim in first inversion from the relative Eb melodic minor and Cb (B) augmented and Db major from the relative Ab melodic minor.

C Minor Jazz/Blues, Melodic Minor

Curt Shumate

STUDY 8. "TRANSYLVANIAN REQUIEM" (HARMONIC MINOR ETUDE) BY JOE STUMP, PROFESSOR

"Transylvanian Requiem" is a piece I recorded as a short instrumental for an Alcatrazz record (2021). The first section is slow and melodic, in the key of B harmonic minor. The classically influenced melody predominantly toggles between the I and V chords (with the VIIdim7 in there as well).

The First Section

While the entire piece is diatonic to B harmonic minor, I use F natural (E♯) in bar 6, and that's borrowed from the B Hungarian minor scale. (Hungarian minor is a harmonic minor scale with a ♯4.) Another noteworthy bit pertains to the very end of the first section where I use a B minor triad arpeggio and add the raised 7 (leading tone) to the triad, along with the 2. I use this violin-style arpeggio quite a bit in my playing/composing. It sounds very classical and is great for cadencing.

The Second Section

The tempo shifts, and the piece becomes more technically challenging. The key also changes to E harmonic minor. The piece starts out with that previously mentioned classical arpeggio containing the minor triad along with the 2 and 7. Another strong melodic classical motif I use in the first two bars of section 2 is what I refer to as a *classical approach-tone sequence*. In this lick, I'm outlining the E minor triad and cadencing to each chord tone with a note a half step away. The piece moves along, with the first four bars repeating. After that, it moves briefly into the E natural minor scale (Aeolian mode). Two-string arpeggios are intertwined with lines from the scale, as the chord sequence moves (Amin, G, D, G).

After that, you have what is without a doubt the most technically challenging two bars in the entire piece: a Spanish-style guitar lick over the V chord (B major) in the B Phrygian dominant scale (the fifth—and by far most commonly used—mode of the harmonic minor scale).

Phrygian dominant goes by many names. Mixolydian ♭9,♭13 would be how many jazz players refer to it), while other players would say Phrygian Major, Gypsy Minor, or Spanish Phrygian. (Note: While "Spanish Phrygian" is often used as a slang term by rock/metal players, technically, Spanish Phrygian contains both the major and minor 3.)

After the vicious B Phrygian dominant lick, the piece returns to the starting melody and finishes out combining a few of the previously mentioned motific ideas.

Transylvanian Requiem
Harmonic Minor Etude

Joe Stump

STUDY 9. "GRAFFITI CEMETERY" (HARMONIC MAJOR GROOVE) BY DAVID FIUCZYNSKI, PROFESSOR

Harmonic major is an exciting and often underused scale system. The harmonic major scale has the following degrees: 1 2 3 4 5 ♭6 7 1, which produces a Maj7(9,♭13) chord. (Avoid the 4, unless you want a susMaj7 sound with a ♭13—also very cool!) There are a lot of wonderful colors in this system, one being the fifth mode: Mixolydian ♭9. This is very useful for tunes from the 1920s and '30s, which often end on a soft Maj6 chord. Mixolydian ♭6 has just enough spice to resolve nicely to a Maj6 tonic without being heavy-handed like altered dominant or Phrygian major. The ♭6 mode is Maj7♯5(♯9), a nice variant for Maj7♯5 chords. The second degree gives you a min7♭5(6/9) chord, an alternative when playing over half-diminished chords.

This study uses the fourth mode of harmonic major. It's very cool if you want to add some spice to those same old min/Maj7 chords we can get tired of! The full chord is: min/Maj7(9,♯11,13). I have often heard how groove players don't want to use advanced jazz chords in their tunes, or how upper extensions get lost when you add some distortion. Well... That's just too bad, and means more toys for me—and you! Check out this melody part and chorus vamp from "Graffiti Cemetery," written by my band Screaming Headless Torsos.

Graffiti Cemetery
Harmonic Major Groove

David Fiuczynski

Melody Part

Chorus Vamp

EminMaj7(9,♯11,13)

STUDY 10. "CHROMATIC TIME" (CHROMATIC SCALE) BY SHERYL BAILEY, ASSISTANT CHAIR

One of the challenges presented to an improvisor is how to create a solo that interprets the harmonic form but is not limited to diatonicism. How can one be clear with expressing "the changes," but use elements beyond playing up and down arpeggios and using scales?

In this study, I've incorporated examples of "simple melodic embellishment" and "extended chromatic embellishment" to outline the basic harmony, as well as the extended harmony of the chord progression of George Gershwin's "Summertime."

The most "simple melodic embellishment" is the use of chromatic notes below the chord tones, and "extended chromatic embellishments" are those that combine various 3 note and 4 note chromatic patterns:

- 2 above/1 below
- 2 below/1 above
- 2 below/2 above
- 2 above/2 below

These patterns can be played in sequence or in varying "permutations" of the note groupings, or even be used to "approach an approach pattern." They are used to target chord tones, as well as chord extensions. Feel free to borrow the ones that you find most intriguing and apply them to your own solos and compositions!

Chromatic Time
Chromatic Scale

Sheryl Bailey

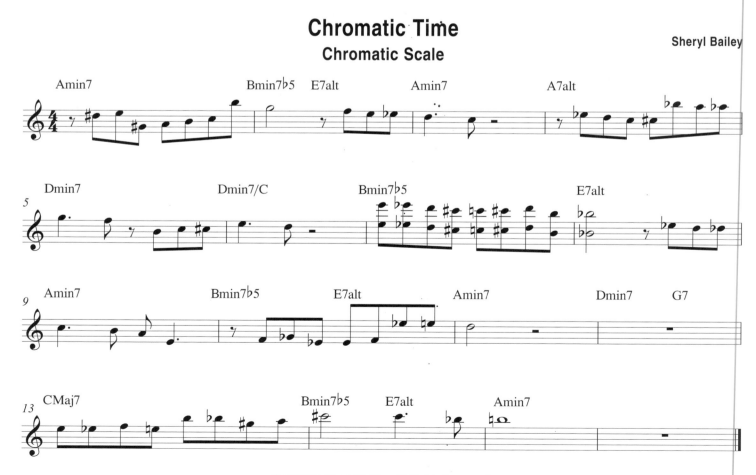

STUDY 11. "WHOLE LOTTA WHOLE TONE" (WHOLE TONE SCALE STUDY) BY RICK PECKHAM, PROFESSOR

The whole tone scale is a symmetrical scale with six notes, each separated by a major second interval. Due to its symmetrical structure, each whole tone scale has six notes, using half of the notes of the twelve-note chromatic scale. As a result, there are only two whole tone scales. Having played one of the whole tone scales, the "other" whole tone scale is found by transposing up or down the interval of a minor second.

Practice the scales by playing the chord, then the scale, with a return to the chord. Listen to the relationship of the scales to the chords and the chords to the scales. Learn this etude! Repeating at a steady, slow tempo will allow you to expand your focus to tone, intonation, and time feel.

Whole Lotta Whole Tone
Whole Tone Scale Study

Rick Peckham

STUDY 12. "DIMINISHED SCALE ETUDE" BY RICK PECKHAM, PROFESSOR

The diminished scale provides a treasure-box filled set of harmonic possibilities. As a quick summary, the whole-step/half-step scale matches well with diminished 7 chords from the root of the chord. The same scale works on dominant 7(♭9,♯9,♮13) chords from the ♭7, ♭2, 3, and 5 of the chord. Musicians who prefer to play from the root of dom7(♭9,♯9,♮13) chords use the other mode of the scale, often called the symmetric diminished scale, which is also often referred to as "half/whole diminished."

Here is a brief etude that explores the application of the whole-step/half-step diminished scale in its application to dominant 7(♭9,♯11,♮13). Bars 9 to 12 feature triad-over-bass-note voicings that can be seen as dim(Maj7) shapes of the most closely related dominant seventh chords shown. Work to play the notated material with smooth fluency.

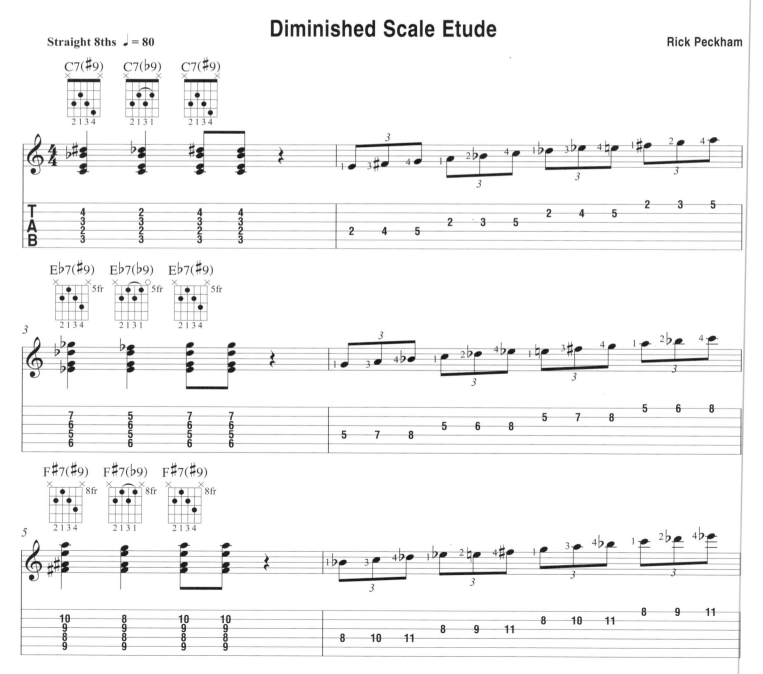

Diminished Scale Etude

Rick Peckham

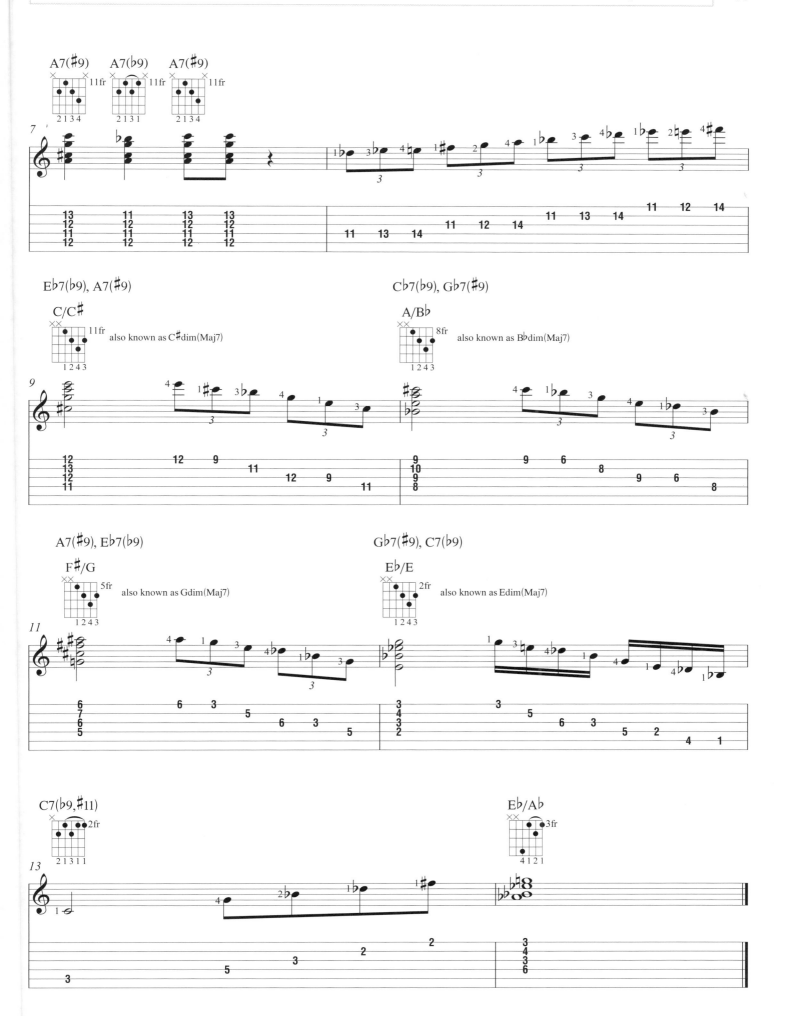

STUDY 13. "CLOSE-VOICED TRIADS" BY JIM KELLY, PROFESSOR

This is an etude written with close-voiced triads. When practicing and performing this piece, try to make the top (highest) note stand out as a melody note. Think of the chords as three voices or three horns. Focus also on a good rhythmic feel. I suggest also making up your own examples—not necessarily complicated, but again stressing the melody and rhythm.

Close-Voiced Triads

Jim Kelly

STUDY 14. "GENERAL SENSE OF WELL-BEING" (FUN USES FOR OPEN-VOICED ARPEGGIOS), BY JON FINN, PROFESSOR

So many times, in private lessons, I'll start talking about spread-voiced arpeggios. Immediately, I go into the nerdiest, most technical explanation of how they work. If the students are polite, they'll do their best to look interested, knowing they'll get a better grade if they at least try. But eventually, as one might expect, the students' eyes glaze over. Why? Because the explanation makes it sound complex. To many, complex equals unmusical. But that's another subject.

So, this is a song I wrote called "General Sense of Well-Being." It appears on my third album, *Wicked* (Jon Finn Group, SEP Music). I was in a bad mood one day, and I heard a story that Beethoven wrote "Ode to Joy" while he was deep in the throes of a dark depression. I knew I wasn't as depressed as LVB, so I knew that writing a song that was "kind of cheery" would probably suffice. This song uses spread-voiced arpeggios and chords all over the place. Can you spot them?

General Sense of Well-Being
Fun Uses for Open-Voiced Arpeggios

Jon Finn

STUDY 15. "THREE-OCTAVE TRIAD ARPEGGIOS STRATEGIES" BY JOHN BABOIAN, PROFESSOR

There are many fingerings available to play arpeggios, and all should be attempted before realizing which ones are going to be your favorites. I found that there is an easy way to play the arpeggios, from any of the degrees, by dividing the six strings into three sets of two strings: ⑥-⑤, ④-③, ②-①. By fingering the three notes of the triad on two strings only, you are able to avoid crossing the dreaded ③-② string crossover! As I hope you are aware, anytime that you cross over those two strings, you have to compensate for the change in tuning. In standard tuning, the guitar is tuned constantly in fourths, except for those two strings that are tuned in thirds. So, if we can avoid the crossover of those two strings, we can use a constant fingering all the way across the neck for a whole three octaves! In the complete three octaves, the last note—the one that completes the last octave—doesn't fit the sequence. That's okay. We can play that note with a remaining finger.

Try following the fingerings. Need the tablature? Sorry, I'm not going to give it to you! At this proficiency level, you should be reading standard notation without too much difficulty.

G Major/Root

E♭ Major/3

C Major/5

STUDY 16. "FOUR-PART CHORD INVERSIONS ETUDE" BY LARRY BAIONE, CHAIR EMERITUS

This piece is an etude that uses inversions of four-part chords. It is based on the old standard tune "On the Sunny Side of the Street." The piece uses chords in root position (root of the chord is the lowest note), first inversion (the third of the chord is the lowest note), second inversion (the fifth of the chord is the lowest note), and third inversion (the sixth or seventh of the chord is the lowest note).

The chords are all drop-2 voicings. Drop-2 voicings are chords that are built by dropping the second highest note of a close-voiced chord down one octave, making that note the lowest note of the chord.

The circled numbers indicate the string on which the lowest note of the chord should be played.

Notice that the dominant 7(♭9) chords—the G7(♭9) in measure 8 and the E7(♭9) in measure 10—have no root. They are diminished voicings that are the 3, 5, ♭7, and ♭9 portions of their corresponding dominant 7(♭9) chord.

In addition to knowing chords and their inversions, it is important to move from one chord to the next in time and smoothly. First, get familiar with each chord voicing in the piece. Next, play each chord and hold for four beats (slowly), and then play the next chord, giving that one four beats. Continue in this way for the rest of the etude. When you are comfortable with moving from one chord to the next, work to play this piece at 60 bpm for the quarter note. Do not just memorize the fingerings: KNOW the chord you are playing.

Four-Part Chord Inversions Etude

Larry Baione

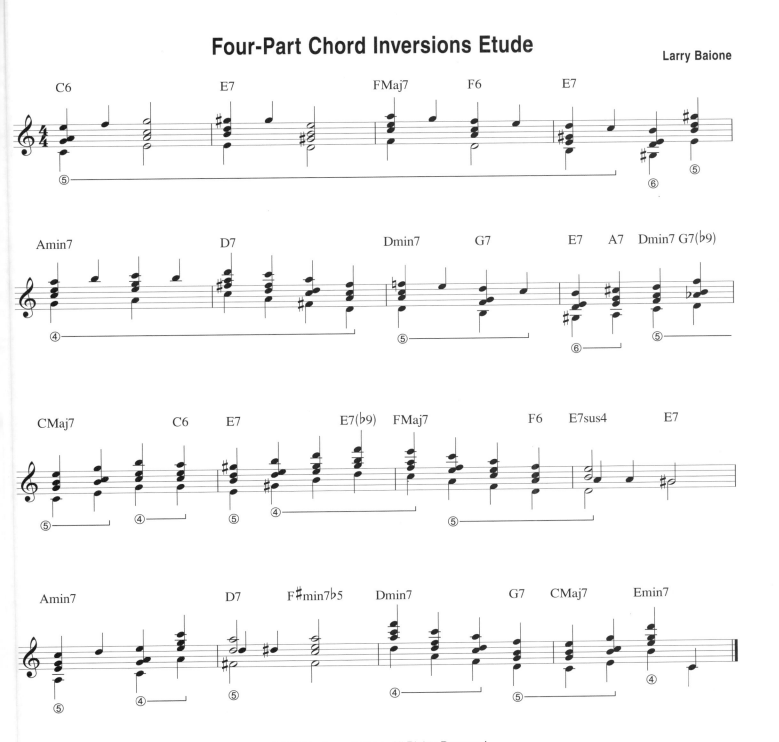

STUDY 17. "MELODIC ETUDE" BY LAUREN PASSARELLI, PROFESSOR

Melodies have never begun for me from scales, theory, or math. Frequencies are sound waves. Sound waves create pitches. I feel into and listen for the right thing when I'm writing a melody, progression, or lyric. I'm always listening to surprise and delight my ears. Hearing music our whole lives develops musical sensibilities that inform our choices. I am reaching for sing-ability and something that I like, and this naturally corresponds to scales, arpeggios, theory, and harmony automatically because that is what music is made of. The emotion, feeling, and resonance is the magic.

Melodic Etude

Lauren Passarelli

STUDY 18. "FUNKY ALBERT" (PLAYING DOMINANT SEVENTH ARPEGGIOS OVER THE BLUES) BY MIKE WILLIAMS, PROFESSOR

The original (or first version) of "Funky Albert" was written and recorded for my book *Blues Guitar Technique* (Berklee Press, 2014), as an exercise/tribute to the great Texas blues guitarist Albert Collins' powerful and unique soloing style. The original take on "Funky Albert" was inspired by his classic instrumental "Frosty," which featured Collins' funky and stinging picking attack and "homegrown" phrases that combine notes from D blues and D pentatonic scales.

"Funky Albert" is also fun to play over while playing more into the chord changes, and that's the approach that was taken for this remake of the solo. While the blues is still the *glue* that ties the phrases together, much of this solo is based on (or around) dominant 7 arpeggios, since they're great for tapping into "chord sound," or the harmony that's sounding at the moment. In addition to playing arpeggios that outline chord tones (chord sound), several phrases also feature tensions of the chord (9, 11, 13, etc.), which can create a wider range of color/textures, and "sweet notes" for the solo, as well.

For guitarists who are working to break out of the blues/pentatonic box and expand their soloing foundation and vocabulary, having a working knowledge of arpeggios such as these may be helpful. To begin, check out the notation and tab for "Funky Albert."

Funky Albert
Playing Dominant Seventh Arpeggios over the Blues

Mike Williams

ABOUT THE AUTHOR

Kim Perlak, the curator of this book and author of its text, has served as Guitar Department chair at Berklee College of Music since 2018, and was assistant chair from 2013 to 2018.

Advisors Larry Baione and Sheryl Bailey serve as chair emeritus and assistant chair, respectively. The members of the Berklee Guitar Department faculty education committee, who contributed studies and ideas for examples in the book, serve on our full-time faculty: John Baboian, Abby Aronson Zocher, Jon Finn, Lauren Passarelli, Robin Stone, David Fiuczynski, Joe Rogers, Mike Williams, Joe Stump, Dan Bowden, Jim Kelly, David Tronzo, Jeffrey Lockhart, Curt Shumate, Rick Peckham, Tim Miller, David Gilmore, Thaddeus Hogarth, and Berta Rojas. The Berklee Guitar Department faculty developed the materials in this book and its applications over the past several decades. For detailed biographical information of all current guitar faculty, please visit: https://college.berklee.edu/faculty/guitar.

ABOUT THE GUITAR DEPARTMENT

Berklee College of Music was the first institution of higher education to grant a degree with guitar as the principal instrument, in 1962. To this day, Berklee's Guitar Department remains the largest and most stylistically diverse guitar program in the world. We provide private instruction, labs, and ensembles in all styles, including: jazz, blues, rock, metal, funk, fingerstyle, classical, world music, modern improvisation, microtonal music, and the avant-garde.

Many of the world's most ground-breaking guitarists studied at Berklee, including Mike Stern, Leni Stern, Kevin Eubanks, Bill Frisell, Gillian Welch, Emily Remler, John Scofield, Steve Vai, St. Vincent, and Adrianne Lenker and Buck Meek of Big Thief. Our alumni community includes current and former faculty such as Mick Goodrick, Pat Metheny, Sheryl Bailey, Wayne Krantz, Tomo Fujita, David Tronzo, and Tim Miller.

To get involved with guitar at Berklee, through formal education in the department at Berklee College of Music, with studies at Summer Programs, through Global Initiatives, or Berklee Online, please visit: https://college.berklee.edu/guitar.

More Fine Publications

Berklee Press

GUITAR

BERKLEE ESSENTIAL GUITAR SONGBOOK
Kim Perlak, Sheryl Bailey, and Members of the Berklee Guitar Department Faculty
00350814 Book...$22.99

BERKLEE GUITAR CHORD DICTIONARY
Rick Peckham
50449546 Jazz – Book..........................$14.99
50449596 Rock – Book..........................$12.99

BERKLEE GUITAR STYLE STUDIES
Jim Kelly
00200377 Book/Online Media............$24.99

BERKLEE GUITAR THEORY
Kim Perlak and Members of the Berklee Guitar Department Faculty
00276326 Book...$24.99

BLUES GUITAR TECHNIQUE
Michael Williams
50449623 Book/Online Audio............$29.99

CLASSICAL TECHNIQUE FOR THE MODERN GUITARIST
Kim Perlak
00148781 Book/Online Audio..............$19.99

COUNTRY GUITAR STYLES
Mike Ihde
00254157 Book/Online Audio.............$24.99

CREATIVE CHORDAL HARMONY FOR GUITAR
Mick Goodrick & Tim Miller
50449613 Book/Online Audio............$22.99

FUNK/R&B GUITAR
Thaddeus Hogarth
50449569 Book/Online Audio............$19.99

GUITAR SWEEP PICKING
Joe Stump
00151223 Book/Online Audio..............$19.99

JAZZ GUITAR FRETBOARD NAVIGATION
Mark White
00154107 Book/Online Audio.............$22.99

MODAL VOICINGS FOR GUITAR
Rick Peckham
00151227 Book/Online Media.............$24.99

A MODERN METHOD FOR GUITAR – VOLUMES 1-3 COMPLETE*
William Leavitt
00292990 Book/Online Media..........$49.99
*Individual volumes, media options, and supporting songbooks available.

A MODERN METHOD FOR GUITAR SCALES
Larry Baione
00199318 Book...$14.99

TRIADS FOR THE IMPROVISING GUITARIST
Jane Miller
00284857 Book/Online Audio...........$22.99

Berklee Press publications feature material developed at Berklee College of Music.
To browse the complete Berklee Press Catalog, go to
www.berkleepress.com

BASS

BERKLEE JAZZ BASS
Rich Appleman, Whit Browne & Bruce Gertz
50449636 Book/Online Audio...........$22.99

CHORD STUDIES FOR ELECTRIC BASS
Rich Appleman & Joseph Viola
50449750 Book $17.99

FINGERSTYLE FUNK BASS LINES
Joe Santerre
50449542 Book/Online Audio...........$24.99

FUNK BASS FILLS
Anthony Vitti
50449608 Book/Online Audio $22.99

INSTANT BASS
Danny Morris
50449502 Book/CD...............................$9.99

METAL BASS LINES
David Marvuglio
00122465 Book/Online Audio.............$19.99

READING CONTEMPORARY ELECTRIC BASS
Rich Appleman
50449770 Book $22.99

PIANO/KEYBOARD

BERKLEE JAZZ KEYBOARD HARMONY
Suzanna Sifter
00138874 Book/Online Audio............$29.99

BERKLEE JAZZ PIANO
Ray Santisi
50448047 Book/Online Audio $22.99

BERKLEE JAZZ STANDARDS FOR SOLO PIANO
Robert Christopherson, Hey Rim Jeon, Ross Ramsay, Tim Ray
00160482 Book/Online Audio...........$22.99

CHORD-SCALE IMPROVISATION FOR KEYBOARD
Ross Ramsay
50449597 Book/CD...............................$19.99

CONTEMPORARY PIANO TECHNIQUE
Stephany Tiernan
50449545 Book/DVD............................$39.99

HAMMOND ORGAN COMPLETE
Dave Limina
00237801 Book/Online Audio............$24.99

JAZZ PIANO COMPING
Suzanne Davis
50449614 Book/Online Audio............$22.99

LATIN JAZZ PIANO IMPROVISATION
Rebecca Cline
50449649 Book/Online Audio $29.99

PIANO ESSENTIALS
Ross Ramsay
50448046 Book/Online Audio $26.99

SOLO JAZZ PIANO
Neil Olmstead
50449641 Book/Online Audio.............$42.99

DRUMS

BEGINNING DJEMBE
Michael Markus & Joe Galeota
00148210 Book/Online Video..............$16.99

BERKLEE JAZZ DRUMS
Casey Scheuerell
50449612 Book/Online Audio............$26.99

DRUM SET WARM-UPS
Rod Morgenstein
50449465 Book......................................$15.99

A MANUAL FOR THE MODERN DRUMMER
Alan Dawson & Don DeMichael
50449560 Book......................................$14.99

MASTERING THE ART OF BRUSHES
Jon Hazilla
50449459 Book/Online Audio............$19.99

PHRASING
Russ Gold
00120209 Book/Online Media $19.99

WORLD JAZZ DRUMMING
Mark Walker
50449568 Book/CD...............................$27.99

BERKLEE PRACTICE METHOD

GET YOUR BAND TOGETHER
With additional volumes for other instruments, plus a teacher's guide.
Bass
Rich Appleman, John Repucci and the Berklee Faculty
50449427 Book/CD................................$24.99
Drum Set
Ron Savage, Casey Scheuerell and the Berklee Faculty
50449429 Book/CD $17.99
Guitar
Larry Baione and the Berklee Faculty
50449426 Book/CD................................$19.99
Keyboard
Russell Hoffmann, Paul Schmeling and the Berklee Faculty
50449428 Book/Online Audio............$19.99

VOICE

BELTING
Jeannie Gagné
00124984 Book/Online Media............$22.99

THE CONTEMPORARY SINGER
Anne Peckham
50449595 Book/Online Audio...........$29.99

JAZZ VOCAL IMPROVISATION
Mili Bermejo
00159290 Book/Online Audio.............$19.99

TIPS FOR SINGERS
Carolyn Wilkins
50449557 Book/CD $19.95

VOCAL WORKOUTS FOR THE CONTEMPORARY SINGER
Anne Peckham
50448044 Book/Online Audio $27.99

YOUR SINGING VOICE
Jeannie Gagné
50449619 Book/Online Audio............$29.99

WOODWINDS & BRASS

TRUMPET SOUND EFFECTS
Craig Pederson & Ueli Dörig
00121626 Book/Online Audio...........$14.99

SAXOPHONE SOUND EFFECTS
Ueli Dörig
50449628 Book/Online Audio..........$17.99

THE TECHNIQUE OF THE FLUTE
Joseph Viola
00214012 Book............................$19.99

STRINGS/ROOTS MUSIC

BERKLEE HARP
Felice Pomeranz
00144263 Book/Online Audio...........$24.99

BEYOND BLUEGRASS BANJO
Dave Hollander & Matt Glaser
50449610 Book/CD.....................$19.99

BEYOND BLUEGRASS MANDOLIN
John McGann & Matt Glaser
50449609 Book/CD.....................$19.99

BLUEGRASS FIDDLE & BEYOND
Matt Glaser
50449602 Book/CD.....................$19.99

CONTEMPORARY CELLO ETUDES
Mike Block
00159292 Book/Online Audio...........$24.99

EXPLORING CLASSICAL MANDOLIN
August Watters
00125040 Book/Online Media..........$24.99

THE IRISH CELLO BOOK
Liz Davis Maxfield
50449652 Book/Online Audio..........$27.99

JAZZ UKULELE
Abe Lagrimas, Jr.
00121624 Book/Online Audio...........$24.99

MUSIC THEORY & EAR TRAINING

BEGINNING EAR TRAINING
Gilson Schachnik
50449548 Book/Online Audio...........$17.99

BERKLEE CONTEMPORARY MUSIC NOTATION
Jonathan Feist
00202547 Book............................$24.99

BERKLEE MUSIC THEORY
Paul Schmeling
50449615 Book 1/Online Audio........$27.99
50449616 Book 2/Online Audio.......$24.99

CONTEMPORARY COUNTERPOINT
Beth Denisch
00147050 Book/Online Audio..........$24.99

MUSIC NOTATION
Mark McGrain
50449399 Book............................$27.99
Matthew Nicholl & Richard Grudzinski
50449540 Book............................$24.99

REHARMONIZATION TECHNIQUES
Randy Felts
50449496 Book............................$29.99

CONDUCTING

CONDUCTING MUSIC TODAY
Bruce Hangen
00237719 Book/Online Media...........$24.99

MUSIC PRODUCTION & ENGINEERING

AUDIO MASTERING
Jonathan Wyner
50449581 Book/CD........................$34.99

AUDIO POST PRODUCTION
Mark Cross
50449627 Book............................$27.99

CREATING COMMERCIAL MUSIC
Peter Bell
00278535 Book/Online Media...........$19.99

HIP-HOP PRODUCTION
Prince Charles Alexander
50449582 Book/Online Audio..........$24.99

THE SINGER-SONGWRITER'S GUIDE TO RECORDING IN THE HOME STUDIO
Shane Adams
00148211 Book............................$19.99

UNDERSTANDING AUDIO
Daniel M. Thompson
00148197 Book............................$44.99

MUSIC BUSINESS

CROWDFUNDING FOR MUSICIANS
Laser Malena-Webber
00285092 Book............................$17.99

ENGAGING THE CONCERT AUDIENCE
David Wallace
00244532 Book/Online Media..........$16.99

HOW TO GET A JOB IN THE MUSIC INDUSTRY
Keith Hatschek with Breanne Beseda
00130699 Book............................$27.99

MAKING MUSIC MAKE MONEY
Eric Beall
00355740 Book............................$29.99

MUSIC INDUSTRY FORMS
Jonathan Feist
00121814 Book............................$17.99

MUSIC LAW IN THE DIGITAL AGE
Allen Bargfrede
00366048 Book............................$24.99

MUSIC MARKETING
Mike King
50449588 Book............................$24.99

PROJECT MANAGEMENT FOR MUSICIANS
Jonathan Feist
50449659 Book............................$39.99

THE SELF-PROMOTING MUSICIAN
Peter Spellman
00119607 Book............................$29.99

ARRANGING & IMPROVISATION

ARRANGING FOR HORNS
Jerry Gates
00121625 Book/Online Audio...........$24.99

BERKLEE BOOK OF JAZZ HARMONY
Joe Mulholland & Tom Hojnacki
00113755 Book/Online Audio...........$29.99

MODERN JAZZ VOICINGS
Ted Pease & Ken Pullig
50449485 Book/Online Audio..........$27.99

SONGWRITING/COMPOSING

BEGINNING SONGWRITING
Andrea Stolpe with Jan Stolpe
00138503 Book/Online Audio..........$22.99

COMPLETE GUIDE TO FILM SCORING
Richard Davis
50449607 Book............................$34.99

THE CRAFT OF SONGWRITING
Scarlet Keys
00159283 Book/Online Audio..........$24.99

CREATIVE STRATEGIES IN FILM SCORING
Ben Newhouse
00242911 Book/Online Media............$27.99

JAZZ COMPOSITION
Ted Pease
50448000 Book/Online Audio.......$39.99

MELODY IN SONGWRITING
Jack Perricone
50449419 Book............................$26.99

MUSIC COMPOSITION FOR FILM AND TELEVISION
Lalo Schifrin
50449604 Book............................$39.99

POPULAR LYRIC WRITING
Andrea Stolpe
50449553 Book............................$17.99

THE SONGWRITER'S WORKSHOP
Jimmy Kachulis
Harmony
50449519 Book/Online Audio $29.99
Melody
50449518 Book/Online Audio $24.99

SONGWRITING: ESSENTIAL GUIDE
Pat Pattison
Lyric Form and Structure
50481582 Book............................$19.99
Rhyming
00124366 Book............................$22.99

SONGWRITING IN PRACTICE
Mark Simos
00244545 Book............................$16.99

SONGWRITING STRATEGIES
Mark Simos
50449621 Book............................$27.99

SONGBOOKS

NEW STANDARDS
Terri Lyne Carrington
00369515 Book............................$29.99

WELLNESS/AUTOBIOGRAPHY

LEARNING TO LISTEN: THE JAZZ JOURNEY OF GARY BURTON
Gary Burton
00117798 Book............................$34.99

MANAGE YOUR STRESS AND PAIN THROUGH MUSIC
Dr. Suzanne B. Hanser &
Dr. Susan E. Mandel
50449592 Book/Online Audio $34.99

MUSICIAN'S YOGA
Mia Olson
50449587 Book............................$19.99

NEW MUSIC THERAPIST'S HANDBOOK
Dr. Suzanne B. Hanser
00279325 Book............................$32.99

Prices subject to change without notice. Visit your local
music dealer or bookstore, or go to **www.berkleepress.com**